Acting On The Absurd

Second Lesson Sermons
For Sundays After Pentecost
(First Third)

Cycle A

Gary L. Carver

CSS Publishing Company, Inc., Lima, Ohio

Copyright © 2001 by
CSS Publishing Company, Inc.
Lima, Ohio

Scripture quotations marked NIV are from the *Holy Bible, New International Version.* Copyright © 1973, 1978, 1984 International Bible Society. Used by permission of Zondervan Bible Publishers. All rights reserved.

Scripture quotations marked NRSV are from the *New Revised Standard Version of the Bible,* copyright 1989 by the Division of Christian Education of the National Council of the Churches of Christ in the USA. Used by permission.

Scripture quotations marked KJV are from the *King James Version* of the Bible, in the public domain.

Library of Congress Cataloging-in-Publication Data

Carver, Gary L., 1946-
    Acting on the absurd : second lesson sermons for Sundays after Pentecost (first third), cycle A / Gary L. Carver.
        p. cm.
    ISBN 0-7880-1829-9 (alk. paper)
    1. Pentecost season—Sermons. 2. Sermons, American. I. Title.
BV4300.5 .C375 2001
252'.62—dc21   2001025096
                                                                                  CIP

For more information about CSS Publishing Company resources, visit our website at www.csspub.com.

ISBN 0-7880-1829-9

Dedicated to:

Christopher Franklin Carver
Kayla Partridge Carver
Bradley Davis Carver
Amy White Carver
Richard Scott Carver
Amy Schwall Carver

A man was never so proud of his three sons
or of the three beautiful women
who love them.

Table Of Contents

Foreword

Gary Carver's life as a minister of the gospel is itself the foreword to his written works. Gary's published sermons reflect decades of digestion and experience. The reader senses that an inquiring mind has wrestled long and hard with the issues in the arena of real life *before* having picked up a pen to connect those issues with his interpretations of sacred texts.

A humble and courteous professional, this book's author pastors a downtown, "First" church which is located near the intersection of several interstate highways. Like his church's location, Gary's office is a junction through which sermon material passes from one destination to another. He avidly and indefatigably collects, indexes, and sorts stories, quotes, and historical experiences. A self-confessed "editor of illustrations," he does far more than clip and paste together well-worn nuggets gleaned from secondary sources. He creates fresh visions forged from the fires of self-reflection and insightful critique. His work is genuine. It is the field journal of a seasoned veteran of the frontline in ministry, the local congregation.

Consequently, the well-illustrated sermons in this volume should be a delight for preachers to utilize. They are not burdened by the noisy impertinence of inexperience. Neither are they saddled with the elbowing self-conceit common to some pastors of large congregations. They are honest, personal, and illuminating. Carver knows how to select and use illustrations that will gain the attention of a congregation and hold it. Mark Twain once wrote that the "difference between the right word and the nearly right word is the same as that between lightning and the lightning bug." The same, I believe, can be said for preachers and their sermon illustrations. The "nearly right" illustration is like selecting the wrong kind of bait for fishing. All the little minnows or perch will keep stealing the bait. Carver's choice of illustrations (his own and others) seems to appropriately match depth with season, temperature, and desired effect. They help him bait his hook to catch the bigger fish. He illuminates texts in ways that reel in the listener without violating the theological meaning intended by the primary authors of those texts.

These sermons also do justice to Pauline theology. Chrysostom, Archbishop of Constantinople in the early fifth century, laments: "I grieve and am pained that all people do not know this man (Paul) as much as they ought to know him." We preachers do not preach from Paul's letters as often as we should. Paul can be hard to read with his extensive use of logic and his innumerable citations from the Old Testament. Gary Carver moves beyond those who find Paul's words to be complex and rigid. He gives to us examples of sermons in which Paul's timeless and deep theological concepts are used to address the struggles of contemporary Christians sensitively. In this respect he has helped us restore the "preachability" of those texts from First Corinthians and Romans.

It should not be overlooked that Paul's emphasis on morality and his assertion that a union with Christ must result in a changed life would have been rather unique in his own day. While such seems perfectly normal to us, religion and ethics were not clearly joined together in Paul's world. The Oriental mystery cults made no practical demands on their followers; correctness of ritual was the essential requirement, not purity of life. Carver has enabled us to appreciate our lasting heritage from Paul, a morally active lifestyle that Paul would call "fruits of the Spirit." Carver's titles cement his understanding of this heritage: "Acting Like God Acts"; "Something That Works"; Acting On The Absurd"; "Free For What?"

From teenage athletes, to contacts in Alcoholics Anonymous, to couples struggling with marriage and a host of other human experiences, Carver profoundly recalls experiences that illustrate Paul's insistence that one can experience a changed life in Christ.

Henry Ward Beecher in his *Yale Lectures On Preaching* (1873) reflected on the task of preaching and left us this profound awareness:

For I still insist that, however needful and appropriate are intellectual equipment and all the accessories of personal bearing, culture and refinement, the prime condition of right preaching is heart and soul; and that to make these right is to keep them in accord always with the bounteous, loving, and all sacrificing, self-denying spirit that was manifested in the Lord Jesus Christ.

Read and use these sermons. The illustrations are appropriate. The intellectual equipment is here. The themes resonate with our culture. Add your own heart and soul to the enterprise and these well-crafted sermons will preach well.

Harold C. Warlick, Jr.
High Point, North Carolina

Preface

These are ten sermons preached during the season of Pentecost without a manuscript before and with a congregation at worship. Of the three feeble efforts I have made at writing a book of sermons, this one was by far the most difficult. One reason that this book was the most difficult is that the majority of the texts are from the book of Romans, which in my humble opinion is the greatest theological document ever penned. It certainly has been one of the most influential. God has spoken through the words of Paul to the church at Rome to such as Martin Luther, John Wesley, and Karl Barth, each of whom began great movements of the power of God charting new waves of church and secular history. Now, *I* am to write a book from Romans! Talk about intimidation! But possibly that is not all bad. Often I felt like removing my shoes before I tried to stand on the sacred ground of the text. That may be a better position than feeling that I owned the text. It allowed me to listen more carefully to that from which so many more able others have heard.

Another reason that this book was most difficult is the deductive, persuasive nature of Paul's arguments. Although filled with doxology, Paul's thoughts here are more emphatic and indicative of his arrival at several destinations. Personally, I am more comfortable with taking a parable of Jesus and guiding the listener along an inductive journey, highlighting interesting spots on the trail, arriving at a mutual destination, each reflecting on what we have experienced. But again this writing task has not been all bad. In fact, in some ways, it has forced me out of my usual homiletical comfort zones and made me exercise a more disciplined and balanced approach to both substance and form. All through this series, I heard in the back of my mind the words of my friend and mentor, Tom Long, who said, "If our preaching is only deductive, the gospel becomes law. If our preaching is only inductive, the gospel is a mystery." Balance ain't bad! Add to that the words of Scott Peck: "Heresy is a good thought taken to its illogical extreme." The same can be said for the use of one particular approach to the exclusion of all others.

In spite of the theological depth and complexity of Paul's thoughts, some of which he left unresolved, I feel that this is a little book of simple sermons, certainly put together by a relatively simple mind. This book evolved out of the simple belief that when we act with faith upon the absurd notion that God loves us unconditionally and wants to share with us his very life — the life of the earthly Jesus — wonderful things begin to happen! When we pull up stakes, as did Abraham and Sarah, we begin the faith journey to our own Promised Land of becoming everything God wants us to be, which is, simply put, more and more like Jesus.

As with my other two books with CSS, *Out From the Ordinary* and *Distinctively Different*, there is no consistent style or form to these sermons. Each sermon draws its substance and form from its respective text, as did the worship services in which they were preached. The nature of the sermons, as already mentioned, is more deductive and didactic. A conscientious effort was made to prepare and present these sermons in a way as to preserve the oral nature of preaching. The congregation at worship was invited to stand and hear the scriptural texts and the sermons were delivered without notes.

I wish to express my deepest gratitude to the family of faith at the First Baptist Church of Chattanooga, the best church of which I know. To be able to share my life and ministry with this loving and hard working group of people is a grace-gift of which I could never be worthy. In our fifteen years together they have given to me far more than they have received.

I also want to express my sincere thankfulness for the worship planning team at First Baptist: Mary Jayne Allen, Clint Scott, John Echols, Jonathan Crutchfield, and Nancy Bowman. Their insight, creativity, and partnership in ministry have made this a better book and me a better minister.

JoAnn Renegar has poured countless hours to the tasks of typing and editing as well as giving wise counsel and unlimited patience. When JoAnn retired, Judy Sullivan took over the unfinished task and completed it with the same thoroughness and dedication.

I especially want to thank my dear and articulate friend, and fellow CSS author, Harold C. Warlick, Jr., for giving graciously of his time to write the foreword. It is a bit embarrassing to me that his foreword is so much better written than my little sermons, but such is the nature of Hal's mega-gifts. I sincerely appreciated his words about the illustrative material. Never much of an orator or preacher, I have enjoyed telling my little stories these last 35 years. His recognition of the value of story and incarnational theology is one of the many points upon which we agree. I also would be remiss without mentioning the "second mile" cooperation of Thomas Lentz and Teresa Rhoads of CSS.

Especially I want to thank my loving wife Sharlon who has put up with my idiosyncrasies, a messy study at home and has given up her Saturday nights for 35 years to allow her procrastinating husband last minute hours to put the finishing touches upon his offering to God for the week. There has to be a special place in heaven for preacher's spouses.

In conclusion, I want to thank my three sons for enduring a workaholic and often pre-occupied father. They have survived being used in sermons as illustrations, an ever watchful eye by some on "the preacher's kids," and empty chairs at ballgames where their father should have been. Through it all they have been the joy of my life, a constant source of encouragement, and friends with whom I have shared the very best of times. I stand with great pride in what they have become and beam with gladness in the three wonderful choices they have made for their partners in life. To these six incredible young adults I wish to dedicate this book.

Lone Rangers
And Cookie Cutters

To be asked to speak or pray in public sent shivers of terror down his spine. He had a small part in his high school play. He froze. When it came time for him to deliver his lines, he could not say a word. He never completely recovered from that humiliation and embarrassment. But if you needed a nurse during a painful or sleepless long night, he was your man. With dozens of people for dozens of years often late into the night, he administered the "sacrament of the coffee pot" as he listened and counseled with a wisdom from a source other than his own. You might say that every developed strength was a detour around or a direct result of a perceived weakness. No one has had more of an influence upon my life. He has a gift and it is of the Holy Spirit.

She felt God calling her when she served in a denomination that frowned upon, if not disdained, women ministers. But at forty years of age she quit her job and went to seminary 300 miles away from husband, home, and family. Two years later, even though she graduated at the very top of her class, she had no place to go. Undaunted, she returned to her hometown and sought out an underpaid part-time job. In eleven years, she carved out a unique ministry for herself, became ordained, and now serves as the Minister of Education in the best church about which I know anything. She has a gift and it is of the Holy Spirit.

He was short, a little overweight, and very poorly coordinated. He had the athletic ability of a hoe handle. He tried out for a baseball team of thirteen and fourteen year olds. He had not a prayer.

15

But instead of feeling sorry for himself, he asked to be the manager. Some said, "Bat boy." But he was much, much more. He worked as hard as anyone. At practice or at a game, he was the first to arrive and the last to leave. He was the team's number one cheerleader. He encouraged everyone. When the team was down, he cheered them up. When they were behind, he challenged them. When the team posted a record of twenty wins with only one defeat and won the city championship, few had contributed more. He has a gift and it is of the Holy Spirit.

These three: one who used failure to find strength; one who persisted in God's call for her life; and the third who simply played the hand he was dealt, stand in stark contrast to two extreme radical attitudes current in the area of spirituality today.

One of these extreme attitudes is the "lone ranger" approach. The "lone ranger" approach to spirituality says that my giftedness and my spirituality are for me. I am independent. The journey is singular and has little or no room for a corporate component. Here one becomes a spiritual snake handler implying that one's gift is superior to another and is used to gather attention to one's self. I appreciate the honesty of a cartoon I saw once of a singer standing before a congregation. He announced, "This song has nothing to do with our worship theme, but it's a wonderful showcase for my voice." There are many dangers in the "lone ranger" approach, not the least of which is the tendency to divorce one's ethics or morals from one's spirituality. I mean, it is my gift, right? What is important is that I express myself, right?

The opposite of the "lone ranger" approach, though not too distant from it, is the "cookie cutter" approach to one's giftedness. The "cookie cutter" approach to spirituality says that everyone is cut from the same mold. Everyone is a carbon copy of the one before. The journey is corporate with little to no room for uniqueness or the freedom of personal expression. Everyone blends into a homogenous blob blindly following a dogmatic authority. Education ceases. Indoctrination is the plan. Dynamic faith bows to creedalism and worship is sacrificed upon the altar of the ritual of sameness. Everyone thinks alike, looks alike, talks alike, believes alike to the radical exclusion of anyone who does not.

16

Somehow, there has to be a balance, a middle ground. There has to be a place where an individual can exercise personal freedom in expressing one's uniqueness and function within a supportive group that accomplishes more together than it would have apart for itself and others. There has to be a place where one can exercise great individual freedom in the context of powerful interpersonal support directed toward a common goal.

That certainly was Paul's desire for the church at Corinth, the most abnormal of all the New Testament churches. In some ways, Corinth was normal, even like some of our cities. People came to this cosmopolitan city from all over the Roman Empire. Much like our own Washington, D.C., Corinth was a center of government and finance. The Isthmian Games were held there, similar to our Olympics. It was abnormal, however, in that many Christians came to their newfound faith from a background of the Greek mystery religions with their sensual practices and often bizarre initiatory rites. Certainly there was carry over from one to the other.

Paul came to Corinth around 51 A.D. and in eighteen months had a church going. As Paul and the young church exchanged correspondence, it became clear that the church's theology was a work in process. They had inquired of Paul his opinion as to what was permissible in worship, as evidently some members were displaying the more showy gifts, such as speaking in tongues, to the bewilderment of those who possessed it not. In order to bring order out of chaos, Paul addresses the situation in chapters 12-14 by beginning with a discussion of the gifts of the Holy Spirit.

He begins by emphasizing that all spiritual gifts have the Holy Spirit as their common source. In fact, no one can even become a Christian unless he or she is wooed and drawn by the Holy Spirit (v. 3). There are different kinds of gifts, different kinds of service and different kinds of working, but the same God works in all of them (vv. 4-6). Then Paul gives a "sampling" list, not an exhaustive one, of spiritual gifts. He not only lists the gifts in verses 7-10, but also in verses 28-31, and in Ephesians 4:11-12 and in Romans 12:6-8 as well. The lists are not identical, which indicates an expansive interpretation of their number. Paul is not trying to limit but expand our field of vision and wants to emphasize that everyone has at least one gift and many have many more.

Every Christian is gifted by the Holy Spirit. Perhaps the key verse to our understanding is verse 7: "To each is given the manifestation of the Spirit for the common good" (NRSV). No one is excluded. Dick van Dyke in his book *Faith, Hope, And Hilarity* tells the story of a woman who takes her five-year-old nephew to church. "Can you genuflect?" she asks. "No," the little boy replies. "But I can somersault!"[1] Some can genuflect and some can somersault, but there is something each one can do.

Several years ago *Newsweek* magazine ran a story in which Stacy King, a professional basketball player for the Chicago Bulls, was quoted as saying, "I'll always remember the night when Michael Jordan and I combined to score seventy points." What Stacy King did not mention is that Michael Jordan scored 69 of those points! But, still Stacy King did score one point and without that one point he and Michael Jordan would not have scored seventy points together. His one point was vital to their joint effort.

Realizing that every Christian has at least one gift, it becomes our responsibility to discover and develop our gift or gifts. We do both by doing. We develop and discipline the gift of music by using it. It is true with our gifts of teaching, leading, caring, earning money for God's purposes, administration, or whatever. As we use them, our gifts grow and we grow in our faith as well.

Grady retired. He had little to do as his wife still worked. With too much time on his hands, he began to associate with some questionable "friends" and on more than one occasion had too much to drink. Living next door to the small church of which he was a member but rarely attended, he noticed a group working to renovate an old Sunday school building. Always handy with a hammer, Grady wandered over and they put his hands to work. Two weeks later he had a new set of friends, helped to organize a work crew for other projects, and later rededicated his life to Christ. He put his gift to work and was more blessed than the church he helped. As Will Rogers once said, "Even if you are on the right track, if you just sit there, you'll get run over." Our gifts grow as we exercise them wherever God calls us to work.

He was the kindest, gentlest, and quietest man I ever knew. Although I was around him a lot, I remember very little of anything he ever said. I do remember him sitting behind a blazing bowl of Carter Hall and quietly reading his Bible. Although he was the last person in the world you would picture doing so, and a painter by trade, he was put in charge of a group of German prisoners of war during World War II. It was his job to plan their work and see to it that they accomplished it. Can you imagine a more difficult task? But he performed his job with such integrity and kindness that they called him "Pops." Prisoners of war called him "Pops"! Now this happened not in Northern Africa or Europe but in Huntsville, Alabama. That man was my maternal grandfather. Not my paternal grandfather. Not the one who was a preacher, or was he?

Thus, we are to use the Holy Spirit's grace-gifts to us wherever we find ourselves for the common good, to make this world a better place and, of course, to build up the church.

Gordon Cosby, of the Church of the Savior in Washington, D.C., states that there is no gift a church needs that God has not given to one of its members. God has gifted every church to do everything he has called that church to do. In fact, God has gifted you to do everything he has called you to do. The Holy Spirit orchestrates all our gifts to be used in unison and harmony to create a beautiful symphony of praise and service to him. Some are trumpets, some are percussion, some are clarinets, others furnish the strings. I am prejudiced toward the trombone, having played one a while back. The piccolo! Do you ever think about the piccolo? Probably not! But just try to play "Stars And Stripes Forever" without it! Every gift is vitally needed in God's great concert of ministry.

I recently called an individual who was attending and showing an unusual interest in our church. "I am a hooker," she said. "Maybe you can use me at the church!" "I, er-uh?" I stammered. "Oh, not that!" she laughed. "I hook rugs the old-fashioned way. Possibly I can teach a night time crafts class." Every gift is important, even that of a "hooker." Some have one gift; some have many. No one has any room to boast. All gifts are given freely, an act of

19

grace, to be used as God wills to carry out his work. You probably have gifts of which you are not even aware.

Derl Keefer states that a discovery has been made that when the roots of trees touch, there is a substance present that reduces competition. This unknown fungus helps link roots of various trees, including dissimilar species. A whole forest may be incorporated together in this manner. If one tree has access to nutrients, another to water, and a third to sunlight, the trees have the means to cooperate with one another to live.[2]

That sounds like the church! That sounds like a middle ground where one can express one's personal freedom and uniqueness yet live with and for each other to benefit the world.

The Holy Spirit gives gifts. William Bausch tells the story of a mother, realizing that two families in their neighborhood were experiencing difficulty, who told her children, "Don't give your father and me anything. Let's try to see that these families have a decent Christmas." One son, Chris, was the basketball manager at his college and was in and out most of the time. In one of his brief visits, as he was walking out the door, he pressed into his mother's hand some money and said, "Take this. It is for those families so they can have a better Christmas." As he bounded out the door, she saw a crisp fifty dollar bill. Aware of the immense sacrifice it took for him to save that amount, she ran after him and jumped into his car. She hugged him. Then for a moment, she was not sitting next to her twenty-year-old son but next to that same son at age five who forgave a friend for stealing his toy car. He said. "Better let me go, Mom, before I start to cry." The mother said, "I love you, honey, and God will bless you for this." "And with that," she said, "I climbed out of the car, leaving with a moment I shall cherish forever; the moment I saw Christ in my son."[3]

The Holy Spirit's greatest gift is Jesus!

---

1. Michael Duduit, editor, *The Abingdon Preaching Annual*, 1995 (Nashville: Abingdon Press, 1994), p. 51.

2. Michael Duduit, editor, *The Abingdon Preaching Annual*, 1998 (Nashville: Abindgon Press, 1997), p. 56.

3. William J. Bausch, *Storytelling The Word* (Mystic, Connecticut: Twenty-Third Publications, 1996), p. 123.

Acting Like God Acts

My good friend, Tommy Garrison, tells the story of a minister who boarded an airplane. He was seated beside a young lady who evidently was very troubled. As the flight progressed, it became even more noticeable that she was upset. In fact, she started crying. The minister said, "I'm sorry. I do not wish to intrude, but can I help you? It seems that you are disturbed." She said, "To be honest with you, I am. I'm flying to California to attend the funeral of my father." The minister said, "Well, from the degree to which you are upset it seems that you were very close." She said, "No. I'm sorry to say that just the opposite was true. We were not close at all. In fact, I had not spoken to my father for over ten years. The last time I spoke to him, my parting words were, 'Go to hell!' " How tragic!

How tragic! Here were two people, members of the same family who no doubt had often shared occasions of affection and joy. How tragic that their last words were of such ill will. Remarkably, the situation between the individuals in Dr. Garrison's story is in many ways similar to the situation to which Paul is writing the "second letter" to the church at Corinth. Having visited the church at least twice and hoping to return for another sojourn, Paul is seeking to pave the way for his return with this epistle. Our text is situated at the conclusion of the correspondence where Paul is naturally trying to say, "Good-bye!" But how does one say, "Good-bye," particularly when the circumstances are varied?

As the reader is aware, there is some disagreement among reputable biblical scholars about the structure and nature of the book of Second Corinthians. Some contend that Second Corinthians is actually a compilation of two separate letters of completely different natures addressed to Corinth upon different occasions. Chapters 1-10 comprise what is generally known as the "thankful" letter, full of joy and gratitude for the young congregation and for their mutual relationship. But with chapters 10-13 Paul's language changes severely. This is known as the "stern" letter written by Paul possibly from Ephesus when his relationship with the Corinthian church was strained, and it may reflect his response to some who were very critical of him. How does one say, "Good-bye"? How does one say, "Good-bye," when the air is filled with joy and gratitude? How does one say, "Good-bye," when there is contention and controversy between the two parties both of whom are aware of the possibility that they may never again meet?

Paul is implying that it does not matter! In the Christian faith and fellowship, one says, "Good-bye," in the same way. It does not matter if you are saying, "Good-bye," to someone with whom you share gratitude or to someone with whom you share hostility. It does not matter if you are hugging or fussing! You say, "Good-bye," in the same fashion because what we have in common is far greater than anything we can ever have in difference. That commonality is expressed in the Trinitarian formula with which Paul closes his correspondence.

This is a triune phrase that most Christians have heard countless times in worship. Notice the order in Paul's closing, "May the grace of the Lord, Jesus Christ, and the love of God and the fellowship of the Holy Spirit be with you all" (v. 14 NIV). Check out the order: Son, Father, Holy Spirit. I will not seek to explain the intricacies of the inter-relatedness of the three persons of the Godhead. For one reason, I do not understand it, and I do not know anyone who does, completely. I do know that some have tried to characterize the Trinity in this way: God the Father is the One who is over us, God the Son is the One who was with us, and God the Spirit is the One who remains with us. Possibly! Another viewpoint would be that God the Father is the God of the Old Testament, God the Son is the God of the New Testament, and God the Spirit is the God of today. Seems a bit strained, don't you think?

Another has tried to describe the Trinity as the Father is the Creator, the Son is the Revealer or Redeemer, and the Spirit is the Companion. That, too, falls incomplete! I think that we are talking about something that is too big for us! But the fact that its complexity is beyond our comprehension should not prevent us from trying to better understand. We are seeking to get the big picture of the wholeness of God, a God who is one in essence and substance, but yet has revealed himself or herself in at least three separate ways or personalities: Father, Son, and Holy Spirit.

I was privileged to study the book of Genesis with Dr. Clyde Francisco as he was re-writing the Commentary on Genesis for the Broadman Publishing Company. In his comments on Genesis 1:26 he stated, "For all that we do not understand about the Trinity, its nature and the different ways in which God reveals himself to us in scripture and today, we know that they always agree." What insight! Thus, the Trinity, the way God acts, becomes a model for the way we should act in the church, thereby finding unity amid diversity and even dissension.

Paul blesses and instructs, "May the grace of the Lord Jesus Christ ... be with you." May the unmerited free gift of Jesus Christ be yours. William Bausch tells the story of a young orphan girl. She was not very attractive and had an edge to her personality that set her at odds with the other children and most of the workers. So severe was her attitude that many prayed that someone would soon adopt her. One day someone noticed as she walked to the fence surrounding the orphanage and she stuck a note in the wiring. The wind blew the note away from the fence, where a stranger picked it up. The note read, "Whoever finds this, I love you."[1] That is what we all are longing for, is it not? We all yearn to be loved, validated, and accepted. We have to know that somewhere, someone cares. Jesus took the initiative and gave to us his unmerited love. Could there be a greater gift? He does not love all of us so much as he loves each one of us. He loves me as I am, and he loves you as you are. He loves you so much that he willingly and intentionally took Calvary's cross to die for your sins. What an absurdly wonderful gift! What an amazing grace! As Paul said in his earlier letter, "For you know the grace of our Lord Jesus Christ, that though he was rich, yet for your sakes he became poor, so that you through his poverty might become rich" (2 Corinthians 8:9 NIV).

Lewis Grizzard relates a story that occurred at the Moreland Methodist Church in which he was reared. On Sunday nights they had a meeting called MYF (Methodist Youth Fellowship). He said that there were two rough boys, really juvenile offenders, in their community who had gotten into trouble. Their punishment as designated by the court was to go to MYF on Sunday nights for six months. That was their punishment! Grizzard said that the first Sunday night they were there they beat up two fifth graders and threw a Cokesbury Hymnal at the woman who was in charge of the group and who brought cookies. She looked the boys square in the face and said, "I do not for one minute agree with what you did, and Jesus does not either, but I guess if Jesus can forgive you, I can too. Sit down, shut up, and eat a cookie!" Grizzard said, "That was the day I saw my first miracle. The last I heard, both those boys had fine families, good jobs, and rarely missed a Sunday."[2]

"My first miracle...." You experienced a miracle the moment you faced Jesus Christ and acted on the absurd notion that he loves us unconditionally. That is a miracle! How do we know the love of God? Because we know the grace of the Lord Jesus Christ. I think that the order is significant here. We know the love of the Father because we know the grace of the Son. "May ... the love of God ... be with you."

In Peter Gomes' excellent book, *Sermons,* he tells a delightful story of a little girl in kindergarten who was very busy drawing with her crayons. The kindergarten teacher passed by and remarked, "My, you are busy. What are you doing?" She responded, "I'm drawing!" The teacher asked, "What are you drawing?" The little girl answered, "I'm drawing God!" The teacher exclaimed, "You are drawing God! You cannot draw God. No one knows what God looks like!" The small student responded, "They will when I get finished."[3]

We know what God looks like. God looks like Jesus. We know that God is good because Jesus is good. We know that God is love because Jesus is love. We know that God's intentions for you are good because we know that Jesus is that way. We know that all of creation is good. The Bible says in Genesis 1 that God looked at creation and said, "It is good!" Then God created you. You are the climax, the crowning accomplishment of God's creation. God made you! Look around. Look at the person next to you. That is the very best God can do! God has made us in his own image. He loved creation so much that he put a little bit of himself into it. He put a little bit of himself in you because you are created in the image of God. We know that God is love because we have seen that love in Jesus Christ.

Tom Lewis is a deacon in our congregation who attends a Business Persons' Bible Study that I teach every Tuesday at noon. Having studied straight through several Gospels, he and I always have the same conversation when we encounter the crucifixion of Jesus. He has a good point! He says that as horrible as it was for Jesus to die upon a cross, suffering the pain, humiliation, and public disgrace, it was even more horrible for the Father because the Father had to stand by and watch his only Son go through it all. Can you imagine how wrenching it was for the Father to see his only Son treated in such a way knowing that He could do something about it, but yet he chose not to? Think how agonizing it would be to see your only child mistreated, abused, and murdered! I cannot begin to comprehend. We know that God is love because we see that love in Jesus, we see that love in the Father who is willing to let his Son die for people such as you and me. "For God so loved the world that he gave his only begotten Son that whosoever believeth in him should never die" (John 3:16).

"May the ... fellowship of the Holy Spirit be with you all." Fellowship! What a wonderful word! We get our word "fellowship" from a Greek root word, *koinos*, which means "common." What does the church have in common? What do we have that binds us together? Certain groups are bound together by various common elements. Some groups are bound together by their views on politics, such as in a political party. Certain groups are built together upon their social status or financial attainment, such as a country club. Other groups are held together by an allegiance to

27

certain values or goals. Some rally around common accomplishments, such as an alumni association. Still others of a lesser nature are drawn toward each other because of common foes or because they hate the same people. Still others have common bonds upon a pure luck of the draw. Parents of twins or other multiple births share a natural affinity.

But what is unique about the church that is different from other organizations? I think that one distinguishing and cohesive factor is that you and I as God's children can stand nose to nose and not have to see eye to eye. The church can be together and not be together. The church at Corinth was together but it was not together. It was known by its decisive schisms. You can tie the tails of two tom cats together and throw them across a clothes line. They will be together but will not be together.

What is unique about the church that binds us together? Several years ago my wife wanted a monkey. I said, "What are you going to do with a monkey? We don't need a monkey." "Yeah, I want a monkey," she said. "Well, if you get a monkey, where will the monkey eat?" "The monkey will eat with us." "We don't need a monkey. Where will the monkey sleep?" "Well, the monkey will sleep with us." "We don't need a monkey. What about the odor?" She said, "Well, I got used to it, so I guess the monkey can too." Sometimes we need to think about what binds us together. We do not need to look at one another. Maybe we need to look at ourselves, and remember that none of us are perfect. I am not. In fact, the great German theologian, Karl Barth, said, "What binds the church together, that which we have in common, is not that which we have but that which we don't have." It is not a positive; it is a negative. We are bound together as the church of Jesus Christ because foundationally we all are sinners and are saved by the grace of God through Jesus Christ our Lord.

It is a deficiency, our common plight as sinners, totally dependent upon God, that binds us together as the church of Christ. That is our common ground. Diverse and distinct we are, yet directed toward a common goal.

We are not only unified because of our common plight as sinners but also unified around our common future goal. A minister of education in our denomination has in his study a plaque that reads, "The main thing is to keep the main thing the main thing." Part of Paul's moral imperatives in verse 11 can be interpreted as, "Stay on the right track." How do we stay on the right track? How do we keep the main thing the main thing? How do we keep the main thing of reaching others for Jesus Christ the top priority? We do so when we realize that we all stand on common ground for a common goal for reaching others for him. We are trying to find a way to reach more people for Jesus Christ. That is our number one priority. We are bound together as we seek to keep the main thing the main thing.

Harry Emerson Fosdick, that great preacher of another generation, tells the story that during World War I, a young man lay dying. A Roman Catholic priest made his way across no man's land to get to that young soldier. As he got there, the young man, still cohesive enough to know that this was a Roman Catholic priest responded, "But, Padre, I do not belong to your church." To which the priest responded, "No, my son, but you belong to my God."[4] That is the foundation of the Church. We have more in common than we can ever have in difference. And when we act like it, we act like God acts.

In 1967, I was privileged to hear Gert Behanna speak at the Southern Baptist Convention in Miami, Florida. Many of her comments were memorable. First, she said that whether a female is eight or eighty, with the menfolk, she always wants to be a "killer"! She also said that the reason most women would rather have beauty than brains is that she knows most men can see better than they can think!

She wrote her life story titled *The Late Liz*. She told that her father was a multi-millionaire, her mother was an international beauty queen, and she was neither. She became an alcoholic. She had never heard the name of Jesus until she was in her thirties, except taken in vain. She told of the wonderful way Christ had transformed her life. She told of how he had taken her from that scared and lonely little girl that never met up to anybody's expectations, who tried to drown her sorrows in a bottle, and changed her into one of the most vibrant and dynamic witnesses I have ever heard.

29

When she finished speaking, over 17,000 rose en masse to give to her a standing ovation. It continued for what seemed like several minutes. She then returned to the microphone and said, "Now you know you ain't applauding an old drunk like me. That is just the Jesus in you meeting the Jesus in me. He doesn't get enough applause. Let's all give him a hand!" Deafening applause erupted.

"The Jesus in you meeting the Jesus in me." Wow! That is fellowship! That is what we have in common that is greater than anything we can ever have in difference. That is what makes us act like God acts!

My dear friend and mentor, Fred Craddock, tells of an occasion when he had several hours to kill while waiting for an airplane. He was told about a church that was located near the airport. When he arrived, he observed that the church was very modest and looked like it had been built by the hands of the people who worshiped there. He said that the sanctuary was very comfortably filled, and as the worship service started, the pastor made his way to the pulpit showing only his left side. He was a very large man and dragged his feet like he was born disabled. His head was immense. Dr. Craddock said that it was easy to tell even at first glance that this was an individual who was very disfigured. Dr. Craddock said, "When he turned to face the congregation, I literally gasped because this was one of the most uncommonly disfigured people I have ever seen. His head was very large and misshapened. His glasses were very thick and one eye sort of looked out into no man's land. When he read, he moved his lips like one who had learned to read as an adult." Dr. Craddock said, "When he started his sermon, he preached on 1 Corinthians 13, the great love chapter. If you had put that sermon on a piece of paper, it would not have been a homiletical masterpiece, but as that pastor spoke to those people, something wonderful happened. You could tell that he was a pastor who dearly loved his people and they dearly loved him. It was a wonderful worship experience; the fellowship of the Holy Spirit was so real; and I was so lifted up."

After the service, Dr. Craddock wanted to take the preacher out to lunch. As he was waiting to speak with the pastor, a lady stopped, shook the pastor's hand, and said, "I wish I had known your mother." The preacher responded, "My mother's name is Grace." Craddock asked the preacher if he could take him to lunch. The preacher already had made other plans. But Dr. Craddock said, "Before you go I would like to ask you a question about your mother. You said that her name was Grace." The pastor said, "It's true. When I was born I was abandoned by my mother and my father because of reasons that are apparent. All of my childhood I was tossed to and fro, from one foster home to another foster home. Nobody really wanted me, because of the obvious. As a youth I heard about a place where people were accepted and loved. I went there and found that people cared for me and people accepted me. The people didn't care what I had been. The people didn't even care what I looked like. They loved me. It was at that place, the church, that I found 'grace.' "

"May the grace of our Lord and Savior Jesus Christ, the love of God, and the fellowship of the Holy Spirit be with you now and forever more."

---

1. William Bausch, *A World Of Stories* (Mystic, Connecticut: Twenty-Third Publications, 1998), p. 330.

2. This story is attributed to Eric S. Ritz of First United Methodist Church, Schuylkill Haven, Pennsylvania.

3. Peter J. Gomes, *Sermons* (New York: William Morrow and Company, 1998), p. 103.

4. Harry Emerson Fosdick, *Dear Mr. Brown* (New York: Harper and Brothers, 1961), p. 118.

Something That Works

Many years ago, a monk was sitting around reading his Bible. No big deal! No earth shattering event! That is what monks are supposed to do, right? I mean, what else have they got to do? And who cares in the first place? So, the world stretched and yawned as this obscure monk sat and read his Bible.

Conceded, this was no ordinary monk. This monk was straining to be monk of all monks with a tireless determination. This monk was striving for perfection with a zeal that was exhausting to himself and exasperating to those around him. This monk fasted until he almost starved. This monk inflicted physical deprivation, even punishment, upon his own body. This monk prayed for hours upon end. This monk confessed his sins endlessly and then confessed his sins some more. This monk confessed on one occasion for six consecutive hours the most trivial of transgressions. This monk confessed so much that the other monks would hide when they saw him coming. This monk once confessed that he had nothing to confess!

When this monk conducted his first Mass, he literally was petrified with fear that he would drop the elements and anger the God whom he felt demanded perfection of him. How does an imperfect monk satisfy a perfection-demanding God? You do everything you can, right? Maybe reading the Bible will help!

So, in a dusty corner of a monastery located only God knows where, an obscure, guilt-ridden monk reads his Bible in a language few of his day could understand or cared to, and this monk's eyes drifted across a line in Romans 1:16, which read, "The just shall live by faith!" And the world was changed! You and I were changed! It was one of the most pivotal events in the history of humankind. It was an event equal to or greater than the signing of the Declaration of Independence. It was an event equal to or greater than Alexander Fleming's discovery of penicillin. It was an event equal to or greater than the Wright brothers' flight at Kitty Hawk. Yes, Virginia, it was an event equal to if not greater than "a small step for man — a giant leap for mankind." A monk read a line from scripture and it changed the world. It changed us all!

A monk read a line from scripture and, as a result, eventually governments would crumble. Rituals and superstition which had enslaved millions for scores of decades were tossed aside like a soiled rag. The most powerful organization upon earth was shaken to its very foundation, never to recover completely. The world was never the same again because Martin Luther ignited the Protestant Reformation. This obscure monk, although he never meant to do so, changed the world when he rediscovered that God's riches and righteousness cannot be imparted through ritual or religion. God's favor cannot be earned, purchased, or paid for! God's love can only be known through a personal relationship with God through faith in the Lord Jesus Christ. What an event! What a monk! What a discovery! "The just shall live by faith!"

Martin Luther discovered, or better yet, rediscovered what someone else by the name of Paul had discovered some 1,400 years before following a similar journey and struggle.

In the first chapter of his letter to the church at Rome, Paul pens these words to a place he has never been, even though it was the center of the known world. Thus, Paul begins by introducing himself and his faith to his potential readers. He wants them to know what he is all about! He wants them to know what his faith is all about. So, at the very onset of the epistle, Paul makes perfectly clear the theme of the letter or better yet, the very essence of his life! It is, "The just shall live by faith." Like the German monk of centuries later, Paul proposes, "I have labored hard and looked a long time and I have found something that works!" Wouldn't you like to have something that *always* works?

My wife and I recently returned from a brief trip celebrating our anniversary. We, that is, I, forgot our camera. So to preserve our precious memories, we bought a 22-dollar throw-away camera. We should have thrown the camera away from the beginning. After two or three pictures, it stopped working.

We built a brand spanking new home several years ago. Everything is new! Everything works, right? Bummer! We had no sooner taken the key out of the lock when something did not work. The microwave did not work. The dishwasher did not work and we had trouble with the HVAC. Oh, for something that always works! Sometimes, we feel like Lucy, complaining to Linus, "Do you want to know what really is the pits? It is having to write thank-you notes for toys that don't work!" Oh, for something that always works!

Paul says, "I have found something that always works and I am excited about it! I can't wait to get there to tell you about the gospel!" The King James Version reads, "For I am not ashamed of the gospel...." Ashamed — Paul? Paul was never ashamed about anything! Not Paul! Not forward, bodacious Paul. Not Paul who "knew" everything. Not Paul who always cut a wide swath. Paul was not ashamed of the gospel even though in his day there were some who were. There were some, especially from a Greco-Roman background, who called the gospel "foolishness." They chided, "You've got to be kidding! You are telling me that an obscure, penniless Jewish carpenter was tried for treason, and crucified as a common criminal by the Roman government, and his death is the key to the meaning of the universe? Absurd!" To many it was pure foolery! It just did not make sense, especially through the lens of those who saw it not through faith. But to those who sorted the story through the eyes of faith, the passion event was the most important happening in the history of the world. It literally was the vehicle through which the true nature of the Eternal God was revealed. No, it did not make sense to many logical minds, but in the ways of God...!

In another translation, Paul says, "I have complete confidence in the gospel" (Today's English Version). In another he states, "I am proud of the good news" (New Century Version). The outstanding biblical scholar F. F. Bruce notes that Paul here is using a figure of speech called *litotes*, a grammatical gimmick in Greek, or "an understatement to underline or increase the effect."[1] Paul is stating his confidence in the gospel in the negative to accentuate the positive. Ashamed? No way! Paul was proud of, had extreme confidence in, gloried in, and could not wait to share the gospel with the church in Rome.

Sometimes preachers have to say something and sometimes preachers have something to say. Paul had something to say about the gospel, because he knew what it could do! He was proud of the gospel because he knew that it was "the power of God for the salvation of everyone who believes ..." (v. 16b NIV).

The English word "power" is translated from the Greek word, *dunamis*, from which we get our word "dynamite." Paul is saying that the gospel is God's dynamite.

In the Old Testament the word "salvation" connotes "wholeness" or "peace." In the New Testament, particularly the way Paul uses the term, "salvation" emphasizes freedom or the deliverance from the bondage of sin and death and its accompanying guilt and shame. In Paul's theology, salvation is an eschatological term which stresses that God's redeeming work in the last days has already begun. No wonder Paul is excited about the power of the gospel. It is a power to pardon our guilt and shame. It is a power to impart a pattern for a new and cleansed life. It is a power to enable us to find God's purpose in this life and a better one in the life to come. The gospel contains the very power to become all God has created us to be. It is the very power to change, or better yet, let God change us more toward the image of his Son. Better than that, the Good News is for everyone — "for the salvation of everyone who believes: first for the Jew, then for the Gentile" (v. 10b NIV).

For everyone? She is nine years old. In her room she listens as the front door opens and closes. Her father has come home for the evening. He is returning from a civic ceremony where he was given the award, "Father of the Year," for the second year in a row. She had stared quietly at her lap through the meal, which always is brief and quieter still. As soon as the meal was over she had asked to be excused. She had gone to her room and locked the door. She knows that very soon she will hear the kitchen cabinet door open and her father will take down his most constant companion, Jack Daniels. She buries her head into the pillow to try to drown out the sounds of her parents arguing and her father hitting her mother. Is the gospel for him?

In his wonderful book, *Habitation Of Dragons*, Keith Miller tells the story of having lunch with a friend when an attractive young woman sauntered up to his table in a pair of very short shorts, sandals, and a brief halter top. She was followed by a tiny daughter in a similar outfit. Miller recognized her as a member of the Sunday school class he taught. After a few moments of conversation she remarked, "I would honestly like to make a commitment of my life to Christ ... but I can't do it. I have a personal problem I can't resolve." Miller responded, "That is why Christianity is called "good news." God gives us the power to cope with the seemingly impossible situations in life. I can't promise to change anything ... just accept his love and grace. We come to him as we are." "Do you believe that?" she asked. "I'd bet my life on it," Miller replied. She looked at her hands for several minutes. "All right," she said, almost as a challenge. "I'm committing adultery every Thursday night with a man who has a wife and several children. And I cannot quit. Now can I come into your Christian family?"[2] Is the gospel for her?

Is the gospel for Jeffery Dahmer or Adolf Hitler or Josef Stalin? Is the gospel for the three men who beat up James Byrd, tied him to a pick-up truck, and dragged him to death? Is the gospel for the Columbine killers? Is the Good News really for everyone? The Bible says, "Emphatically, yes!"

The gospel is for everyone because everyone has sinned. "All have sinned and come short of the glory of God" (3:23 NIV). All of us and each one of us have done things we should not have done and left undone things we should have done. All have sinned! In Paul's thought, sin is not only what we do or do not do, but a state in which we find ourselves because we are less than what God intended because of our personal rebellion to his will for us. As I try to teach the children in our membership classes, "Sin is when I want what I want more than I want what God wants." That is sin! We all are guilty.

The great evangelist of another era, Billy Sunday, was preparing to preach a revival campaign in one of our large cities. He wrote to the mayor and asked him to send a list of people who possibly had spiritual problems or who were in need of prayer. Billy Sunday was surprised when the mayor sent back to him a copy of the city telephone directory. All have sinned! Thank God that the gospel is for all of us.

Paul continues by saying that he is excited about the gospel not only because he knows what it can do, but also because he knows how it works! It works through faith! "For in the gospel a righteousness from God is revealed, a righteousness that is by faith from first to last, just as it is written: 'The righteous will live by faith' " (v. 17 NIV).

If someone presented the challenge to create a new world or even a new person, that challenge could be met with various responses. Some would say, "Learn!" Education is the key. If a man or woman knows what to do, they will do it. Knowledge is the answer. Change is brought about with the mind. Others would say, "Earn!" Money is the key. If you have enough money, you can correct the woes and wrongs of society, or at least, you can live with them more comfortably. Financial power is the answer. Change is brought about with the dollar. Others would say, "Burn!" Radical change is the key. You must tear down and destroy the old ways, quit your habits, and start all over. Revolution is the answer. Change is brought about with the scythe. These are three tested ways, suggested by some, to bring about change. The only trouble is, they are not biblical. The Bible says, "Turn!" Repentance is the key. We must turn from our sins and turn toward God. Nothing less than a 180-degree turn will do. Conversion is the answer. Real, lasting change is brought about through the heart. Only we cannot do it! Only God can through the power of his Good News.

There is only one way to come to God and that is through Jesus Christ. We come to him when we act on the absurd notion that he loves us unconditionally and turn from our sin and turn to him in true repentance and allow him to change us. Paul states,

"That was my experience. I was on the road to Damascus to gather Christians to be persecuted, and God struck me blind and helpless. There was nothing I could do because I could do nothing. I was totally dependent upon God. In my helplessness, I was able to say I was wrong. I was wrong to think I could earn my way to God. I was wrong to detest this new way to God called Christianity and to persecute its followers. All I could do was to say that I was wrong and place my childlike faith in the Lord Jesus and depend upon his power to change me. My faith was my own, not second-hand or borrowed from tradition. My faith was personal, not an adherence to a creed or gathered through ritual or religion. I realized that I did not have to be perfect because I could not. I realized that I did not have to depend upon my own righteousness because I had none. I only had to realize that I was a sinner and that God loves and saves sinners and makes them brand new."

C. T. Studd went to hear the evangelist Dwight L. Moody because he had lost a bet. A socialite, he cared nothing for religion and went with no positive expectations. But he heard a man who seemed to pierce his very heart. C. T. Studd was converted to Christ. He only lived two years after his conversion, but many said that he put more into those two years than many Christians put into a lifetime. An individual who worked for him said it best, "All I can say is this: There was the old skin on the outside, but there was a new man on the inside."[3] That is how God's gospel works. We put our faith in him and he makes us brand new. Thank God for something that always works!

That kind of radical change and complete reversal sounds extreme, even painful. And it is! There is only one thing more painful and that is the unwillingness or the refusal to do so! It was said of Lyndon Johnson that he never felt he had the luxury of re-examining his position once he fully committed the nation's full resources to Vietnam. Never re-examine? Never change? Never correct a wrong? Never repent? And thousands of lives were lost because one man could not change direction. It costs a lot to say, "Yes," to God. It can cost even more to say, "No."

When we say, "Yes," God's dynamite always works. Aren't you glad that there is something that works every time? Why?

Because its working is not dependent upon us but upon God. Our salvation is not dependent upon our rites, rituals, and religion, but upon God. We aren't saved by our faithfulness, but his! We are not delivered by our good works, but by Christ's work on the cross. "Great is thy faithfulness, O God our Father." As Dr. Frank Stagg translates verse 16, "The righteous live by faith in the faithfulness of God." It is God's work, pure and simple, from start to finish. We are totally dependent upon the love and grace of God.

Dr. Stagg goes on to say that the phrase "from faith to faith" (v. 17) can also be translated "from a lesser faith to a greater faith." In short, it gets better! We grow! Our faith grows as God shares with us his very life, his very nature as we grow to be like Christ. God is faithful! God can be trusted to keep his word. "Therein is the righteousness of God that is revealed" (v. 17a). This is a righteousness that is an attribute of God — his very life and character. This is a righteousness that is an activity of God, putting us in right standing with him which enables us to share his very life. God's righteousness is both a pattern for our life and a power to live the life he wants us to have.

God can be trusted! Ask a nineteen-year-old nervous novice squirming anxiously in his seat trying to discover a scriptural text upon which to preach his first sermon in October of 1965. His eyes, too, drifted across those words, "The just shall live by faith." "That's it!" he cried! "That is the Christian life! That will be the text for my first sermon." I was that young preacher. I am here to tell you that after over 34 years and thousands of sermons, I have never once found God to be lacking or his promises to be deficient. In every circumstance I have always found God's word sufficient and his promises never failing! It works and it gets better. God can be trusted. Ask me. I will tell you.

Or ask Dennis Simmons. He came to hear my very first sermon. He was my best friend. My hero — All-State Center in football, and he was not a Christian. At the conclusion of the little sermon, that big mound of muscle came forward, shook my hand and made the best profession of his childlike faith of which he was capable. Ask Dennis! It gets better. Today he is a dynamic

Christian, has a beautiful wife and family, and is the assistant Superintendent of Education in our home county. Ask him! Dennis will tell you that it gets better. God can be trusted.

William J. Bausch relates a story told by the man who served as the Bishop of Notre Dame in the early part of the 1900s. He told the story of a young man who would stand outside the cathedral and shout derogatory slogans at the people entering to worship. He would call them fools and all kinds of names. The people tried to ignore him but it was difficult.

One day the parish priest went outside to confront the young man, much to the distress of the parishioners. The young man ranted and raved against everything the priest told him. Finally, he addressed the young scoffer by saying, "Look, let's get this over with once and for all. I'm going to dare you to do something and I bet you can't do it." The young man shot back, "I can do anything you propose, you white-robed wimp!"

"Fine," said the priest. "All I ask you to do is to come into the sanctuary with me. I want you to stare at the figure of Christ, and I want you to scream at the very top of your lungs, as loudly as you can, 'Christ died on the cross for me and I don't care one bit.'"

So the young man went into the sanctuary and screamed as loud as he could, looking at the figure, "Christ died on the cross for me and I don't care one bit!" The priest said, "Very good. Now do it again." And again the young man screamed, with a little more hesitancy, "Christ died on the cross for me and I don't care one bit!" "You're almost done now," said the priest. "One more time."

The young man raised his fist, kept looking at the statue, but the words wouldn't come. He just could not look at the face of Christ and say those words again. The Bishop continued, "I was that young man."[4]

It works and it gets better! Ask me! Ask Dennis! Ask the Bishop at Notre Dame. It works! Or better yet, ask yourself! Does your personal faith work for you?

1. Dale Moody, *Romans, The Broadman Bible Commentary*, Volume 10 (Nashville: Broadman Press, 1970), p. 167.

2. Keith Miller, *Habitation Of Dragons* (Waco: Word, 1970), pp. 69-71.

3. James E. Hightower, Jr., *Illustrating Paul's Letter To The Romans* (Nashville: Broadman Press, 1984), p. 11.

4. William J. Bausch, *A World Of Stories* (Mystic, Connecticut: Twenty-Third Publications, 1998), p. 244.

**Proper 5
Pentecost 3
Ordinary Time 10
Romans 4:13-25**

Acting On The Absurd

In his stimulating book, *The Dynamics Of Belief*, the beloved former pastor of the First Baptist Church of Chattanooga, Don Harbuck, tells the story of a thirteen-year-old boy. Life for this young lad had been difficult. He and his younger brother had not only suffered through the loss of their mother, but they had borne the burden of an alcoholic father and his abject irresponsibility. In fact, the two boys often had nothing to eat. They lived on the berries they picked and the rabbits they killed and cooked over an open fire. Life for them was difficult, at best.

Once a neighbor had paid them 75 cents to cut wood all day. They had worked hard for the money and were headed to the store to buy food for their empty stomachs when their father intercepted them and demanded the money. What else could they do? They gave the money to their father, who then went to buy whiskey. That night the younger boy went to bed hungry. The thirteen year old left home for good. He found a job in a nearby city washing dishes all night in a restaurant and barely eked out a living.

Later in his life when friends would invite him to church, he hesitated to go because someone would always use the word "Father" for God. Every time he heard that word "Father," something at the very depth of his soul grew hard and frozen.[1] Is God like that? Father God? What kind of God is God and can he be trusted?

A while back a denominational religious leader made the statement that a certain city in Florida had better be aware, because God might send a tornado through their town. It seems that a small group of people in that city made a decision with which the so-called religious leader did not agree. Now let me get this straight! Let's think through that. God is a God who sends tornadoes upon entire cities, levy's punishment on unknowing bystanders, destroys homes, and kills innocent children for a decision with which they had nothing to do! Is God really like that? What kind of God is God, and can he be trusted?

William Barclay, the great New Testament scholar, lost his daughter and son-in-law in an automobile accident. An individual wrote to him, anonymously, of course, and said, "I now know why God took your daughter. It was to save her from your heresy." Barclay wrote, "If I could have spoken to that person I would have said, 'Your god is my devil.' " Is God like that? What kind of God is God and can he be trusted? Can we really trust God?

I was in a shopping mall a few years ago talking with a four-year-old African-American boy who was as cute as a speckled pup. We were having a big time passing the time while his mother and my wife shopped. I would grin at him and he would grin at me. I would wave at him and he would wave at me. I would laugh and he would laugh back. We were having the best time. I reached into my pocket, took out one of those little mints that I always carry and tried to give him one. No! No! He backed off. He would not take the candy. On the way home, I sorrowfully told my wife that he would not take my candy. She said, "He has been taught not to trust strangers." I said, "I'm no stranger. I'm me." She said, "Believe me, you are stranger than you think." What kind of God is God and can he be trusted?

Not coincidentally, those are the very questions that Paul was addressing in his letter in our text. Paul says boldly, triumphantly, and without a shadow of doubt, "God is a God who can do anything." *God is a God who can do anything?* Verse 17 is probably one of the greatest faith statements in all of the Bible about the power of God. Paul says, "For God is a God who cannot only give life to the dead, but God is a God who can create something where there is nothing." God can take nothing and make something out of it. God not only can give life to the dead, but God can take nothing and make something out of it.

We've all heard the little jingle: "We have done so much for so long with so little we now qualify to do anything with nothing." Well, God can do anything with nothing. He has shown it! God has shown that he can create something out of nothing in creation. God is the God of creation. God created the vastness of our universe out of nothing! The fancy theological term is *ex nihilo*. God created everything out of nothing. The Bible says that only God can create. Man can fashion, man can control, man can manipulate, but man can create nothing! In Genesis the Hebrew word for "create" is *bara*, and is reserved for God alone.

The law of the conservation of mass and energy states that "matter can neither be created nor destroyed." It may change form from solids to liquids or gases, but cannot be created or destroyed. Only God can do that. God can create something out of nothing. God can even give life to the dead.

Paul states that God proved that he could make something out of nothing in the lives of Abraham and Sarah. Against all hope, Abraham in hope believed and so became the father of many nations, just as it had been said to him, " 'So shall your offspring be.' Without weakening in his faith, he faced the fact that his body was as good as dead — since he was about a hundred years old — and that Sarah's womb was also dead" (vv. 18-19 NIV). Abraham was 100 years old and Sarah was ninety. This old couple was tired, weary, worn out, and half-dead. They were not considering the purchase of a new home near a nursery school! Write over their maternity hopes the word "ABSURD." There again is where God comes into play. Here God shows that he can give life to the dead by giving to those almost lifeless bodies new life in the form of their son, Isaac! No wonder they called their son "Laughter." Absurd! Impossible? Not with God!

But again God showed himself to be the master of the impossible as he took a slain carpenter, called a traitor by the state, and returned him to life after he had been stone-cold dead for three days. God raised Jesus from the dead! Our God can not only take nothing and make something out of it, he can also take the dead and give them life. Our God can do anything!

45

A bird, the golden plover, lives in the winter in the Arctic and travels in the summer to South America, a distance of 8,000 miles. At one stretch that bird flies 2,500 miles non-stop. How does the plover know the way? If God cares that much for a bird and guides that bird in such an ingenious way, how much more can he guide you — his child, made in his very image? How much more does God care for you? God is a God who can do anything.

In 1968, my wife and I left Gadsden, Alabama, borrowed 200 dollars and set out for The Southern Baptist Theological Seminary in Louisville, Kentucky. I was in desperate need of a job. Our desperation was made more so by the fact that Sharlon was pregnant with our oldest son, Chris, and we had an 85-dollar medical insurance premium due any day. I journeyed to the state employment office. "We have an opening at Central Hospital," they said. "I'm not choosy. I can work in a hospital," I replied. I went to Central Hospital in Anchorage and to my surprise, found that it was a state mental hospital. "See Jim Collins," they said. I went to see Jim Collins. "Well, Gary, already they have called from the employment office and said that you have experience working in a hospital. I am glad to hear that!" said Jim Collins. "No, Mr. Collins, I do not have experience working in a hospital of any kind, much less a mental hospital." I tried to make it clear. A few days later, Jim Collins called, "Gary, I just wanted you to know that the job is between you and another person, but because of your experience, I am preferring you." "No, Mr. Collins, I promise you that I have never worked in a hospital." Two days later Jim called, "Gary, you have the job." The first day I reported for work Jim Collins said, "Gary, it is good to have someone of your experience on our staff!" "But, Mr. Collins...."

God can create what he wants to create, even if it is misunderstandings to get what he wants done. God is not only One that can do anything, God is a God who can be trusted. Romans 4:19-21 states: "Without weakening in his faith, he faced the fact that his body was as good as dead — since he was about a hundred years old — and that Sarah's womb was also dead. Yet he did not waver through unbelief regarding the promise of God, but was strengthened in his faith and gave glory to God, being fully persuaded that God had power to do what he had promised." Abraham believed that God could be trusted to fulfill his promise. Can you not see the absurdity of it all? This old couple, weary of rocking an empty cradle, wondering how to bounce a baby boy on bony knees are told, "Got a promise for you. Leave your land because I am going to make you parents of a passel of people." And they went — half dead and 100 years old! No heir — no future — just a promise — and they left!

"Where are we going?" "I don't know?" "How will we know when we get there?" "I don't know!" So they set out on a long, weary, hot and dusty trip to only God knows where. Each day of the journey there were tents to put up, animals to tend, mouths to feed. No doubt Sarah said to the old man, "Abraham, can't we stay a few days here? Just tonight I would like to get out my best china, the linen table cloth, some cloth napkins, huh, Abraham?" "No, Sarah, just use the paper plates and styrofoam cups. We have to leave early in the morning." No rest for the weary. Gotta move on. Such is the journey of faith.

Then there was that day when Abraham and Sarah were going through another ordinary dusty day in the desert when they entertained angels unawares. Angels? Yes, angels who reiterated God's promise that Abraham and Sarah would have a little boy — at their age — a child? Sarah laughed. Who wouldn't? That was ridiculous, absurd, impossible. Maybe that's why the Lord did it, to show that this birth could have occurred in no other way except through the activity of God. I mean, this God can do anything! And he does not have to have perfect people through which to do it. Remember the episode at the genesis of the journey when Abraham lied about Sarah being his wife out of fear for his own skin? No paragon of virtue, this guy. Maybe that is one of the reasons why God chose to use him.

But Abraham did have his good days, some exceptional. After the boy was born and bonding made, God asked Abraham to offer him up. "Take him to Mount Moriah," God commanded, "and offer him as a sacrifice to me." Tough command. But in possibly his finest day, Abraham takes his only son, the heir to the promises for which he had lived his life and stumbles up the mount, heavy with the demand placed upon him. "Where's the sacrifice, Daddy?" Little Laughter asks. "God will provide," the old man answers. And God did. If you could summarize the life of Abraham, it might be found in Genesis 22:19, "God will provide." Here is not only a God who can do anything, but One who can be trusted to provide. God said to Abraham and Sarah and to all the Abrahams and Sarahs since, "Trust me!" And God says to us, "Trust me. I will provide."

A minister in the northern part of the United States has her office wall papered with a special paper. Every space is filled with the words, "Trust God! Let go! Trust God! Let go!" God is saying to us today, "Trust me! Let go!" God can be trusted.

Max Lucado has two daughters, Andrea and Sarah. Little Sarah loves to jump off the bed into his arms. He tried one night to get her to jump off the bed into the arms of the older sister, Andrea. "Jump off the bed into Andrea's arms." She would not do it. "Why won't you jump into Andrea's arms?" She said, "I only jump to big arms."[2]

God asks us to exercise a little faith and jump into his big arms. He is a God who can and will provide for us as he did for Abraham and Sarah.

In verse 17, Paul states that Abraham knew "in whom" he had believed. In the original language there is an intriguing play on words. The words "in whom" can also mean "over against." Here is a beautiful image of Abraham standing over against God or face to face with God. Thus, Abraham could trust God because he had a personal relationship with God face to face. Same with us! Paul adds, "That's why it is said, 'Abraham was declared fit before God by trusting God to set him right!' But it's not just Abraham; it's also us! The same thing gets said about us when we embrace and believe the one who brought Jesus back to life when the conditions were equally hopeless"[3] (vv. 22-25). It is nothing for our God. He majors on the ridiculous, the absurd, the impossible!

Perhaps Zig Ziglar gives to us a picture of what this looks like in his true story of Little Annie. Things were seemingly hopeless for a young girl locked in manacles in the dungeon of a mental institution just outside Boston a number of years ago. She was called "Little Annie." Even though this institution was one of the more enlightened ones for its day, the doctors felt that a dungeon was the only place for those who were "hopelessly" insane. So Little Annie was consigned to a living death in a small cage that received little light and even less hope.

About that time, an elderly nurse in the institution was nearing retirement. She felt there was hope for all of God's creatures, so she started taking her lunch into the dungeon and eating outside Little Annie's cage.

In many ways, Little Annie was like an animal. On occasions, she would violently attack the person who came into her cage. At other times, she would completely ignore the person. When the elderly nurse started visiting her, Little Annie gave no indication that she was even aware of her presence. One day, the elderly nurse brought some brownies and left them outside the cage. Little Annie gave no hint she knew they were there, but when the nurse returned the next day, the brownies were gone. From that time on, the nurse would bring brownies when she made her Thursday visit. Soon the doctors in the institution noticed a change was taking place. After a period of time, they decided to move Little Annie upstairs. Finally, the day came when this "hopeless case" was told she could return home. But Little Annie did not wish to leave. The place had meant so much to her she felt she could make a contribution if she stayed and worked with the other patients.

Many years later, Queen Victoria of England, while pinning England's highest award on a foreigner, asked Helen Keller, America's First Lady of Courage, "How do you account for your remarkable accomplishments in life?" Without a moment's hesitation, Helen Keller responded, "I could not have accomplished anything if it had not been for Teacher, Annie — Little Annie — Annie Sullivan — the miracle worker."[4]

It truly is amazing what can happen when we act on the absurd promises of God. As Tertullian, the early church father said, "We must believe it, because it is absurd."

———————

1. Don B. Harbuck, *The Dynamics Of Belief* (Nashville: Broadman Press, 1969), p. 37.

2. Max Lucado, *When God Whispers Your Name* (Dallas: Word Publishing, 1994), p. 101.

3. Eugene Peterson, *The Message: The New Testament In Contemporary Language* (Colorado Springs: Navpress, 1993), p. 312.

4. Zig Ziglar, *See You At The Top* (Gretna: Pelican Publishing Company, Inc., 1972), pp. 113-114.

Rightwised

I knew that I was wrong with God and that I was scared. I was only nine years old. I had not robbed a bank. I was not a serial killer. I had not shaken a defiant fist in the face of God. I was only nine years old, but I knew I was wrong with God and that I was scared. I knew I was wrong with God because I knew I was a sinner as evidenced by the fact that I had stolen a piece of chewing gum from my mother's purse that very morning. Not big stuff, you say, but after all, I was only nine years old. But I was old enough to know I was a sinner and that my sin had created a separation between me and God.

I was scared. A few weeks earlier I had dreamed that I was on the roof of Mike Galloway's clubhouse where we often played. I looked into the sky and saw Jesus coming back to earth again, and I knew that I was not ready. I was scared.

On that morning God sent a preacher to hold a revival at our church, from of all places, Chattanooga, Tennessee. His name was Ansel Baker. I remember many things from that Sunday morning sermon. I remember that Ansel Baker said that he had a "red" Bible because he thought the Bible ought to be "read." He particularly caught my interest when he said, "If you are scared that God is going to send you to hell, forget it!" Whew! "Thank you, Lord," I said to myself. "Now I don't have to do anything." But then he quickly added, "You'll send yourself." "Uh-oh!"

Dr. Baker offered an invitation "to accept Jesus." From my vantage point of the second pew, I saw two men hugging each other in front of the church. My father later mentioned something about the two of them in a court battle over a property line dispute. I only knew that something was happening and that I needed to do something. So, I went forward and gave my hand to Sidney Argo, our pastor. I became right with God. I gave as much as I knew of myself to as much as I knew of God. That wasn't much! I was only nine years old. But that moment changed my life. Nothing I have ever done in all my life has ever influenced me more than that single decision to follow Jesus Christ as my Lord and Savior. I have not always lived up to my part of the bargain. Many times I have fallen woefully short, but God has never failed me. I came to God out of ignorance and fear, and he gave to me far more than I ever imagined on the day I became right with God. Did I tell you that I was only nine years old?

In the fifth chapter of Romans, Paul is talking about all the wonderful things that God gives to us when we become "rightwised" — right with God.

We rejoice in a new relationship to God (vv. 1-2). Notice that verse 1 begins with a "therefore." It is an important word. When you see a "therefore," ask, "Why for the therefore?" "What is the 'therefore' there for?" The "therefore" serves as a connecting word or bridge between the concepts of chapters 1 through 4 and the concepts of chapters 5 through 6. The word could be rendered "as a result of." Paul is saying, "therefore," "as a result of" having realized that Jesus died for our sins, repented of our sins and in child-like faith put our trust in God, absurdly wonderful and joyous effects are brought about by God in our lives.

God has justified (v. 1) us by his grace through faith. Our word "justification" comes from a Greek word which simply means "to put right." Our word "righteousness" also is built on this Greek root and always refers not to something we are or have earned but to a position imparted to us. Christ has put us in "right standing" with God. Justification is a descriptive word which has a forensic or legal background. It paints this picture: A man stands before the judge. He is undeniably guilty and stands ready to receive the punishment he deserves. The judge says, "There is no doubt as to your guilt, thus, you shall die." The condemned man proceeds to the gallows to face his sentence. As he is about to ascend to the gallows, a court messenger arrives and declares, "Wait, even though you are guilty, the court has granted you a pardon. You are free and returned to a right standing with the law 'as if' you had never committed the crime." Christ pardons us "as if" we had never sinned and reinstates us to himself with full privileges. Frank Stagg calls this "an acquittal that brings life."

Romans 5:1-8 is a beautiful description of the many gifts God gives to us when he "puts us right" with himself! Therefore, we rejoice in a new relationship with God characterized by his peace (v. 1). Before, our lives were characterized by an enmity or hostility between ourselves and God caused by our own sinfulness. Now, because we are put right with God by faith, we have a serene, deep peace that comes from the hand of God. This is a peace akin to the serene settledness of deep ocean waters unaffected by surface noise and commotion. It is a peace that results from the knowledge that our sins are forgiven and our relationship to the Father is restored.

History records the fact that in the War of 1812, Andrew Jackson and his troops defended the city of New Orleans against the British and won. Unknown to Jackson and his men, however, the battle was fought weeks after the peace treaty had already been signed in Europe. Because of the slowness of communications, hundreds of soldiers died for a peace that had already been secured. Just as great a tragedy is the fact that today many are suffering in sin when possible peace with God has been secured.

We rejoice in a new relationship to God characterized by an *access* to him (v. 2a). Before, in the old covenant, access to God was very limited. Only the high priest went into the holy of holies and then only once a year. Now, because through Christ's death the veil of the temple was "rent in twain," we have unlimited access to the throne of grace. We have been "put right" with God and now come before God as an invited and honored guest.

It is said that upon a significant battlefield in Korea, a sign was posted which read, "The precious blood of the gallant officers and men of the Seventh Calvary Regiment makes it possible for you to be here." There should be a sign posted at the throne of grace reading, "The precious blood of Jesus Christ hath made it possible for you to be here." We not only have peace with God but direct access to Him. In that we rejoice.

We rejoice in a new relationship to God characterized by *hope* (v. 2b). Before, when still in our sin, we were hopeless, lost, with no future — no purpose or direction to life. Now we can know the direction of our personal pilgrimage — we are headed toward Christ-likeness! We are going to be like Jesus and share in his glory. "Christ in you, the hope of glory!" God is working in our lives to make us to be "conformed to the image of his son" (Romans 8:28-29 NRSV).

When I was a student at The Southern Baptist Theological Seminary in Louisville, Kentucky, one of our finest chapel speakers was D. E. King, an African-American preacher from Chicago. Someone asked Pastor King why black Christians were always joyful in their worship, even when things were not going well. The pastor exclaimed, "We rejoice in what we are going to have."[1] Allow me to enhance that by saying because of our hope in Christ, we rejoice in what we are going to be — like Jesus. Because of being "put right," we have a new relationship to God characterized by peace, prayerful access, and hope.

We rejoice in a new understanding (vv. 3-5). Because we have been "rightwised," we can better deal with difficulty.

There is an old tombstone in upstate New York with an epitaph which reads: "In memory of Ellen Shannon, aged 26, who died March 21, 1870, when she was burned to death from an explosion of a lamp that was filled with R. C. Danforth's non-explosive burning fuel."[2] "Non-explosive burning fuel?" Something that was not supposed to explode did and took Ellen Shannon's life. This is the world in which we live. We are subject to the random results of an imperfect universe. Christians have no protective shield nor are immune to the harsh realities of life. In fact, suffering is part and parcel of the Christian experience and sometimes is even caused by our Christian stance. We, as Christians, live in, not apart from, a world that is wrong with God. Just because we are right with God does not mean that we are immune to what is wrong with the world. But Paul assures us that we can rejoice, even in our sufferings. How? He shows us how.

We can rejoice in our sufferings because we know that God is working in our lives to produce endurance (KJV — patience, v. 4) from tribulation. The word translated "tribulation" can better be rendered "pressure." Are you feeling the pressure of everyday life? Are you suffering under the harsh pressure of financial problems, marital problems, sickness, vocation, or family problems? Take heart! Here's good news! The word translated "endurance" comes from two words which mean "to stay under." When life caves in, God gives us staying power, the ability to stay under, to hang in there.

Recently I was with Judge George Carpenter, one of the finest Christians I know. He told of a recent time of testing following a tragic accident. "I felt as if I had come to the end of my rope. You know what I did? I tied a knot in the end of the rope and hung on!" That's the "endurance" God gives, the ability — his ability — to hang in there. But this is not a passive and placid acceptance of whatever may come. Inherent in this concept is the active effort to overcome.

We rejoice because we know that endurance produces character (KJV — experience, v. 4). The word in the original language connotes a quality of being tried, tested, and approved. In trying to get through college, I worked three summers at Republic Steel in Gadsden, Alabama. It was amazing to see how they seemingly could pour about everything in the world — scrap iron, rocks, minerals, and so on, into those huge furnaces. Then the heat of the fire would do its work and out would come a pure, hardened, tempered, and tested steel product exactly fit for its intended purpose. God uses the fires of testing in our lives to burn out the impurities and to temper and mold us to be fit for his use!

We can rejoice because God uses character to produce hope (v. 4). The natural result of such endurance and character is an optimistic attitude of hope. We know that God will not disappoint us in our hope (v. 5a) because he has given to us the Holy Spirit as a guarantee (v. 5b). He is our assurance, our down payment, that our hope is not in vain and that we are never alone.

It is said that during World War II, a squad of American soldiers befriended a group of hungry and destitute orphans in Europe. The

Americans did everything they could for the nourishment and security of the children, but they still could not sleep at night. The soldiers then happened upon a remedy for the restlessness of the children. In the hand of each child before retiring for the night was placed a piece of bread. The children slept soundly, knowing that they would eat tomorrow. The bread was their guarantee that they would not be hungry. The Holy Spirit is God's guarantee that our hope is not in vain and he will be with us supplying our every need according to his riches. As Romans 8:32 states, "He who did not spare his own son, but gave him up for us all — how will he not also, along with him, generously give us all things?" (NIV).

And what does he wish to give us? The very life of Christ, himself. I do not want a changed life. I want an exchanged life. I want to exchange my old life for the very life of Jesus, one filled with peace, access to the Father, hope, and growth in suffering.

Such a life is possible for us today, because God loved us enough to send his son to die for us even while we were still sinners (v. 8). He gave his life for us even though we might never know about it or might even reject his overture of love. As I look at my own children and grandchildren, I ask myself, "Would you be willing to give up one of those precious lives for someone who might never care?" Hardly! But Christ died for sinners, like you and me!

When I was nine years old, I was wrong with God and I was scared. But I came to God and asked him to put me right with him. God did. God gave to me far more than I ever imagined or will ever discover. He will do the same for you. There is a tale told about a fatherless family, a mother with two sons, living in the South during the Depression. Life was hard. The mother had one thing of which she was very proud, her big, fluffy feather bed. The sheets were always white and crisp. The bed was always immaculately made. The boys had the run of the house except for that bed. Nobody was to get on mother's feather bed with those big, beautiful fluffy white pillows and those clean, crisp sheets.

The youngest son came in the house from the outside where he had been playing in the yard. He hardly noticed the mud on his bare feet. As he walked by the bedroom, he saw the big, beautiful white feather bed with the big, white fluffy pillows. He thought, "This is my chance. Brother is out mending a fence and mama is in the barn. Nobody will ever know." Then he thought, "Oh, no, I can't do it." Then he thought, "Oh, yes, I can!" So the lad scampered into the room. He mounted the headboard and did a beautiful swan dive right into the middle of his mother's feather bed. He was having the time of his life. He was jumping joyously and punching the pillows. He was having so much fun that he lost track of time. Then, he looked up and out of the corner of his eye he saw his mother standing in the doorway. She had in her hand a hickory stick, slapping it up against her leg. He thought. "Oh, no, I'm in for it now." Then out of the corner of his other eye he looked and saw his older brother standing in the window. His brother then did a beautiful and wonderful thing. He climbed in through the window, edged toward his younger brother, and ascended over his brother on all fours, encasing him, and he said, "Mama, I know he deserves it. He has done wrong and I want you to really lay it on him. But I'll take it for him this time." The mother stared as her chin began to twitch. She then dropped her switch. "Get out of here before I whip you both," she said as she wiped a tear from her cheek.

Would it be improper to say that while we were yet sinners, Jesus said, "I'll take it for them this time?"

---

1. James E. Hightower, Jr., *Illustrating Paul's Letter To The Romans* (Nashville: Broadman Press, 1984), p. 36.

2. *Preaching,* Volume V, Number 5, March-April, 1990 (Jacksonville: Preaching Resources, Inc.), p. 46.

Buried, But Alive

Baptism is a solemn, sincere, often serene, significant service of Christian worship. But sometimes it is so serious that it is just down right funny. The late Bob Baggott used to tell about baptizing a new convert to his congregation by immersion. As he lowered her under the water, he discovered that she had not informed him that she was wearing a wig that was then floating on top of the water as she descended under it. Baptists traditionally have not believed in dancing, but he said, "She and I danced all over that baptistry trying to scoop her up under that hairpiece!"

It has not been too many years ago since I baptized an exuberant and energetic eleven-year-old girl, who promptly after coming up out of the water dove back under and swam enthusiastically out of the baptistry! Oh, the reckless joy of youth!

I conducted my first baptism in 1966. He was a dear friend who was married to another dear friend whose marriage was in deep trouble. "She has left me," he said as we talked in my driveway after his surprise visit on an early Sunday morning. "It is mostly my fault," he said, hoping that getting his life right with God would help enable them to get back together. He professed Christ and I baptized him the following Sunday. Shaking my hand as he left the church, he remarked, "Whether she comes back or not, I now feel I can handle it." She did not and he did.

One of my most memorable baptisms occurred as I served the East Huntsville Baptist Church in Huntsville, Alabama. They were an elderly couple who had recently moved from Ohio. She joined. He did not. He told me that he had never joined any church. After about a year, most of it spent battling cancer, he strolled down the aisle in his wheelchair, tearfully professing, "I want to give what little is left of my life to Jesus." Two weeks later it took four of us to get him out of the chair and into the water. I conducted his memorial service six months later. At the funeral his wife remarked, "There has not been a day in which he has not spoken about what his baptism meant to him."

I am thankful that our congregation has taken giant strides in beginning to recognize the significance of baptism. We now ask our baptismal candidates to write out a brief testimony and to ask an individual of special significance to read it for them. I have seen grown men silenced to tears as they struggle to read the words of their son or daughter. I have seen other adults, teachers, uncles, grandparents, beam with joy in recognition of the part they played in introducing the candidate to Christ.

It is said that the early church made much of the symbolism of baptism. They often baptized in the Jordan River where Jesus was baptized facing Jerusalem where he was resurrected. They often baptized on Easter Sunday. It was said that the candidate was often given brand new clothes to wear, symbolizing the death to the old life. Sometimes they were given milk and honey to eat symbolic of the entrance into the new life of the Promised Land.

I remember my own baptism. I was only nine years old and remember very little of the service. I am sure that Brother Sidney Argo said all the right things about being buried with Christ in baptism and being raised to walk in newness of life. I was concerned about other things. Was I going to be baptized before or after Mike Galloway, my best friend at the time? I was concerned whether I had enough dry underwear. I am positive that I did not understand the full significance of that moment, but I have spent the last 45 years of my life contemplating what my baptism has meant to me. I hope that you, even now, are remembering your baptism — who baptized you — who was there and the difference it has made in your life. Remember your baptism! Is that not what Paul is exhorting us to do in verse 3 of our text, "Don't you know that all of us who were baptized were baptized into his death?" Earlier Paul said, "But God demonstrates his own love for us in this: While we were still sinners, Christ died for us" (5:8 NIV). He goes on to say, "Consequently, just as the result of one trespass was condemnation for all men, so also the result of one act of righteousness was justification that brings life for all men" (5:18 NIV). Buried with Christ in baptism, raised to walk in newness of life! In baptism grace has reigned over death and sin.

Paul continues, "Shall we go on sinning so that grace would increase?" (6:1 NIV). Of course not! God forbid! Being buried with Christ means that we are dead to sin! Radical statement. Is it true that we sometimes play down the radicality of baptism symbolized by total immersion? Being put totally under the water symbolizes being totally dead to sin, does it not? James McBride, in his wonderful book, *The Color Of Water*, relates the experience of receiving a letter from his mother. It began, "I'm dead." Her decision, as an orthodox Jew, to marry his father, a non-Jew, rendered her, in the eyes of her tradition, as totally dead. Her decision completely cut her off from her old life. Is this what Paul means when he said in verse 11, "In the same way, count yourselves dead to sin..."? What does it mean to be "dead to sin"?

Does being dead to sin mean that we no longer sin? Of course not! Paul later said in chapter 7, "We know that the law is spiritual; but I am unspiritual, sold as a slave to sin. I do not understand what I do. For what I want to do I do not do, but what I hate I do. And if I do what I do not want to do, I agree that the law is good. As it is, it is no longer I myself who do it, but it is sin living in me. I know that nothing good lives in me, that is, in my sinful nature. For I have the desire to do what is good, but I cannot carry it out. For what I do is not the good I want to do; no, the evil I do not want to do — this I keep on doing." No longer sin? Heavens, no! Paul confessed to being the "chief of sinners" and that was after his conversion to Christ.

Does being dead to sin mean that we no longer find sin attractive? Again the answer is in the negative. In fact, Martin Luther complained that the devil had the best music. Is that the reason why he took what some labeled a "bar tune" and penned to it the words of "A Mighty Fortress is Our God"? It was said of William Gladstone, the Prime Minister to England's Queen Victoria, that he was the most righteous man in all of England and the most boring! Does being dead to sin mean that folly has lost its allure or attraction? Hardly! In some ways, we may find it even more attractive. There is something about "forbidden fruit."

Does being dead to sin mean that we no longer have the desire to sin? No! Often we have even more of a desire to try that which we are not supposed to do. Tell me I cannot have something, and I never realized how badly I wanted it until I was told I could not have it. Vanilla ice cream with chocolate syrup looks even better when I am on a diet.

We should have known it was a mistake — a big mistake! Several years ago we bought our twin sons solid white suits for Easter. They were about five years old. On Easter Sunday after my wife dressed them for church in those clean white suits, she said, "Do not go out in those clean white suits. Do not go out and get dirty!" The moment she said that, their little eyes lit up as if to say, "Thank you, Mother, we had not thought about that!" Of course, as soon as she turned her back, they were out the door with gratitude for the suggestion.

Does not Paul echo the same sentiment in chapter 7, verses 7-8: "What shall we say, then? Is the law sin? Certainly not! Indeed I would not have known what sin was except through the law. For I would not have known what coveting really was if the law had not said, 'Do not covet.' But sin, seizing the opportunity afforded by the commandment, produced in me every kind of covetous desire. For apart from law, sin is dead" (NIV). What does it mean then to be dead in sin if we still sin because we still have the desire and the attraction for the forbidden? I think that the symbolism of baptism encompasses the fact that we are made dead to sin and are raised to walk in a total newness to life. We are totally immersed. We are totally raised to walk in a new way. The Bible describes conversion as a new birth. We are born again from above. We put on Christ. We are clothed with Christ (Galatians 3:27). We are baptized into his death and participate in his resurrection. Paul states in 2 Corinthians 5:17, "Therefore, if anyone is in Christ, he is a new creation; the old has gone, the new has come" (NIV). A new creation has emerged living a new life in Christ. Paul states his case plainly in verses 5 and 8, "Now it is God who has made us for this very purpose and has given us the Spirit as a deposit, guaranteeing what is to come. We are confident, I say, and would prefer to be away from the body and at home with the Lord."

"Raised to walk" with Christ means that we now live our lives in union and fellowship with him. To borrow a phrase from Keith Miller, we now live our lives "to an audience of One"! It means that we have crucified the old self and are no longer enslaved to sin. Sin no longer has dominion over us. We now have a choice.

My first year in seminary, I worked at the Central State Hospital in Louisville, Kentucky. One of my co-workers was a middle-aged man by the name of John. John invited me to attend an Alcoholics Anonymous meeting in which he was receiving a special award. This pastor's son was receiving recognition for one year of sobriety. He stated so eloquently, "I now know that there is a power greater than my alcoholism and that power is God. In Him, I have the power to say no!" When we are raised to walk in our new life in Christ there is set loose in our lives a power that is greater than any of our sins. Thus, we sin because we choose to sin. What happens when we continue to sin, as we all do? Well, life takes on the flavor of an artist's studio instead of a spelling bee. In a spelling bee, one misspelled word and you sit down. One mistake and you are out! It is like going to the plate with two strikes already against you. However, in an artist's studio the atmosphere is different. The artist makes a mistake, a bad stroke, and she starts over. In the artist's studio the work is forever in the making.

We are forever a work in process. We have the power through Christ to say, "No," to sin, not to be controlled or enslaved by sin but to have power and freedom over sin. It means we have a choice, and it means that we pay the price for our choice. There is a responsibility.

Many of you remember Edgar Bergen. Before he was famous as Candice Bergen's father, he was famous as a ventriloquist with his side-kick, Charlie McCarthy. The story goes that Edgar Bergen, George Burns, and Jack Benny went to lunch. When the waiter came with the check, Jack Benny said, "I'll take the check, please." Jack Benny was given the check. As they left the restaurant, George

Burns turned to Jack Benny and said, "That was real nice of you to take the check." Jack Benny said, "I didn't ask for the check, but that's the last time I'm going to lunch with a ventriloquist."[1]

I love that story. But just the opposite is true. We have been buried with Christ. We have a choice and we have to take responsibility for our choices. If we order the meal, we pay the check. That's the bad news! The absurdly good news is Christ died for our sins!

For many years Troy Morrison was the Executive Director of the Alabama Baptist State Convention. Prior to that, he served as the pastor of the Twelfth Street Baptist Church in Gadsden for seventeen years. During his pastorate there, he was once approached by a member of his congregation who asked, "Pastor, if ever anything happens to me, would you see that my children are cared for?" He, like most pastors in such an awkward moment, responded, "Well, of course I would." Within two years, the mother and the father both had died. Troy and his wife prayed and decided that they would honor his word to take care of the woman's children — all four of them — two teenagers. There also were matters of a large hospital bill and funeral home bill for the mother's service. Word circulated about the Morrison's generous gesture.

Within a few days Troy received a letter in the mail from the president of the Baptist Hospital. Enclosed was the mother's hospital bill. Across the bottom it read, "Paid in full!"

The next week Dr. Morrison conducted a funeral service for another congregant. As he and the director of the Collier Butler Funeral Home were riding to the cemetery, the funeral director reached into his inside coat pocket, with tears in his eyes, and handed Troy an envelope. Inside the envelope was the mother's funeral bill. Across the bottom it read, "Paid in full!" That is what Jesus did for us! He paid the price for our sins — in full!

His name is Jan Douglass. Two years before he had pitched his team to the Little League World Series in Williamsport, Pennsylvania, where they placed third in the world. He never lost a game. On July 4, 1960, he was taking the mound as our starting pitcher as we were playing for the Gadsden Pony League City Championship in a game that received press in *The Gadsden Times*

25 years later. Both teams sported identical 19-1 records. Douglass' only defeat was to his mound opponent that day, Macky Moates, in a crushing 12-3 shellacking. Over 10,000 fans crowded the ball park standing four deep around the outfield fence. As the visiting team, we were first at bat and unexplainedly scored four runs without the benefit of a hit. Before he threw a pitch, Douglass gathered the entire team around him as we took the field for the bottom half of the first inning. Jan said, "When the game is over, we are going to carry Coach Gallager around the bases." To him, turn out the lights, the party was over! School was out! The game was won! And it was. He also clouted a mammoth home run just to accent his prediction. Oh, the other team scored a few runs, but to Jan Douglass, we already were City Champions.

We still have to play the game, but the outcome is secure. The other team will score a few runs. We will strike out every now and then or make an error or two, but the game is over — victory is assured. Christ — and we — win! We share his life! We share his victory! We are now alive in Christ! "The death he died, he died to sin once for all; but the life he lives, he lives to God. In the same way, count yourselves dead to sin but alive to God in Christ Jesus" (vv. 10-11 NIV).

When Major Ian Thomas spoke in one of my churches years ago, he wrote in the front of one of his books he presented to me: "All there is of Christ is available to the man who is available to all there is of Christ!"

He is ours!

We are his!

We share his victory!

Peter Gomes was my friend and teacher at Harvard Divinity School. He tells a wonderful story in his book, *Sermons*, of a baptism he was asked to conduct as the minister of the Memorial Church. A young, undergraduate couple came to him and said, "We want to be baptized." As he heard their request, he said, "I will be glad to do it." But there was a problem. They wanted to be immersed and the Memorial Church at Harvard has no baptistry. He said, "All the bowls in the world couldn't do that." So they said that they had a special fondness for Walden Pond — yes, that

Walden Pond. So on an October morning in New England the three of them went to Walden Pond with some blankets, some liquids (coffee, I'm sure) to keep them warm, and a Bible. The place was deserted. The three of them went into the water. He said, "I remembered how it was down, down and up, down and up." He said, "I baptized the woman last. As she came up out of the water, all of a sudden from behind us we heard a round of applause."

Somehow a group of people had gathered to see what in the world three people were doing in Walden Pond in the middle of October. He turned and explained to them that this was a baptism and this was what Christians do. He used some scripture to explain about baptism, and then one of them said, "Well, how often do you do this?" Peter Gomes answered, "Not often enough." Then that person who didn't know what in the world they were doing said, "That sure looks like fun." [2]

Baptism should be fun — serious, but yet fun! It should be joyful and celebrative. Why not? The most wonderful thing that can happen in the life of an individual has happened. We have been buried with Christ in baptism and are raised to walk in the newness of his life.

---

1. Charles L. Allen, *The Secret Of Abundant Living* (Old Tappan, New Jersey: Fleming H. Revell Company, 1980), p. 60.

2. Peter J. Gomes, *Sermons* (New York: William Morrow and Company, Inc., 1998), p. 33.

Free: For What?

Belmont Abbey College in North Carolina sits on property that was once a large southern plantation. The land was given to the Roman Catholic Church and they built an abbey and college on the property. The monks found a huge granite stone on that property upon which men, women, and children stood centuries ago and were sold as slaves. The monks took the stone and hollowed out a hole in the top and carried it into the abbey's chapel, where to this day it serves as a baptismal font. The engraving on it reads: "Upon this rock men were once sold into slavery. Now upon this rock, through the waters of baptism, people become free children of God."[1]

Free children of God! Free! But what does it mean to be a free child of God? It is to this question that Paul addresses himself in chapter 6. In verse 6, he states, "For we know that our old self was crucified with him so that the body of sin might be done away with, that we should no longer be slaves to sin" (NIV). No longer slaves to sin — we have been set free! We now have a choice. We now have the ability to say no to sin because there is a power unleashed in us that is greater than sin's control. No longer are we a helpless pawn blown about by every shifting wind. We have Christ's power within us through his victory over sin. Now we can win the victory over sin's control. But beware! Our newfound power of choice brings with it an accompanying responsibility.

We no longer have an excuse! We no longer can affix the blame to anyone or anything else. As Paul states in verse 14, "For sin shall not be your master ..." (NIV). We now have the power to say,

"No," to take matters in our own hands and to take responsibility for our own actions. No longer can we blame our environment or our parents or poor potty training. No longer can we hide under the excuse that the government is at fault. Or the church! That's it! It's the church's fault. Or vice versa, the devil made me do it! We no longer can blame anyone! We are at fault! We can only blame ourselves. We sin because we choose to sin. We deny God's ability in us to win the victory over sin. We are responsible for ourselves because God has placed within us his power to choose good over evil. Sin does not have to be our master. We can let his grace reign in us as a free child of God.

Now the question remains, "Free, for what?" What shall we do with this marvelous gift of freedom that God has placed within us because of Christ's victory on the cross? Paul says that we are free *not* to do certain things. We are free not to be partial Christians. We are free not to hold on to different parts of our lives as if they did not go through the baptismal waters. We remember that in the book of Romans the word "sin" not only includes individual acts of sin but speaks about a general direction for our lives. When we are headed in a direction, we don't go back. That is why Paul is saying, "Do not offer the parts of your body to sin as instruments of wickedness but rather offer yourselves to God." Part of our bodies? They say during the Middle Ages when a soldier was baptized, often the soldier held his right hand out of the water. He would not allow his right hand to go under the baptismal waters because that soldier knew if that right hand was baptized he could no longer kill.

What kind of baptism would that be if one deliberately and intentionally held back part of oneself from God? A partial Christian? A contradiction in terms! But think a moment! Are there areas of our lives that we are seeking to conceal or withhold from God? Are there rooms in our house that we keep locked and hidden from view? Is there a secret closet? Is there a part of our lives that has not been baptized? What about our pocketbook? Did our wallet get wet? What about our leisure time? Is God the Lord over the books we read, the movies we see, the recreational places we attend? What about our stomach? Do we allow God to help us discipline our appetite for food? What about our appetite for sex? Some seem to think we can divorce our commitment to Christ from our moral ethical decisions. Did we allow our driving habits to be baptized? (Ouch!) Do we allow God's power to operate in us in that we give our families proper respect, energy, and attention? Are there areas where we still want to hold on to old habits and ways? Do we have parts that we held out of the baptismal waters? How would you complete this sentence? Jesus is the Lord of my life except for _____!

In Philip Yancey's wonderful book *What's So Amazing About Grace,* he tells the story of Big Harold. Big Harold was a strong influence in Yancey's young life. Known for his impeccable morals, Big Harold was stern and strict. He used the Bible like a weapon to keep people in line. Harold was obsessed with morality. He often complained about the United States being too permissive, even to the point where he moved to another country to flee from the U.S.A.'s moral self-indulgence. It was in this other country that he found a job censoring books and magazines, much to his legalistic liking. He even started a church where he was the pastor. Again his contempt of permissiveness prevailed as he forbade young people in his church to chew gum, pass notes, or even whisper during the sermon.

Yancey decided that he would pay Big Harold a visit. Big Harold's family met Yancey at the airport, but no Big Harold. "Where's Big Harold?" The faces of embarrassment were evident. Big Harold was not there because he was in prison for running a pornography ring at the very same time he was the stern and autocratic pastor! A porno ring? How in the world could that be? How could one be so strict and stern but yet have one area of one's life so totally unyielded to God — an area of one's life that stood in direct contrast and contradiction to everything else for which one seemingly stood? How could this be?

The prayer group of which I am a member recently studied the Yancey book. One member commented upon Big Harold's hypocrisy, "Big Harold's radical extremism was a defense mechanism to cover up the fact that he felt inferior. He felt that he had never been loved and saw himself as unworthy." Does our group member have a point? Possibly so. Perhaps Big Harold felt so unloved that he lived a fragmented life. His life was so disconnected that he could blot out one area of his life and completely remove it from all the others. God does not want us to be fragmented or partial Christians. He baptized all of us. He put to death the old life completely and raised us to walk in the complete newness of his life. Sin should not be our master. We should not be fragmented or disconnected. Christ has made us whole.

We should not settle for a partial faith or a puny one. That's right! A puny one! We should not settle for one half or part of the Christian life. Fred B. Craddock has stated that one of the biggest faults he hears in sermons today is that they are puny. They are little, thin, and have no size. Can it be true that sometimes little preachers proclaim a puny God restricted to one's own small experience or particular creed? Do we sometimes arrogantly argue as if God is in our back pocket and can operate only under the confines of our experience, theology, denomination, or circle of friends? Is our God too small, our perspective too narrow, our vision exclusive? Do we have a puny faith?

Again Yancey is helpful. He states that often in the churches of his particular background much energy and emphasis were placed upon the length of one's hair, whether one should wear jewelry, or listen to rock music. Never was heard a word about racial injustice, the plight of blacks in the South, or the horrors of the Holocaust. He said that they were too busy measuring the hem length of skirts to say a word about nuclear war or world hunger. If it is true that we perceive a puny God and practice a puny faith, then often we come to church only to express our likes and dislikes, as if our experience is the only way God's activity in the world can be interpreted.

Paul is stating in verse 13 that we have not been brought through the waters of baptism to settle for a partial or puny faith. In verses 16 and 17 he continues to emphasize that we have not been given new life through baptism to recede into the past. "Don't you know that when you offer yourselves to someone to obey him as slaves, you are slaves to the one whom you obey — whether you are slaves to sin, which leads to death, or to obedience, which leads to righteousness? But thanks be to God that, though you used to be slaves to sin, you wholeheartedly obeyed the form of teaching to which you were entrusted" (vv. 16-17 NIV). We must not revert to old habits or reach back and drag along that which does not belong to our present Christian experience.

One day Paul Harvey was talking about modern day Russia. He said that the people have no idea what to do with their newfound freedom. Some have romanticized about the old days of Communism and desire to return to their former slavery. Others have no personal discipline or morals and have looted over 30,000 valuable art works. Freedom can be a frightening thing when one does not know how to handle it.

Paul states that God has not saved us to go back into our old life and drag it along like a heavy burden. God has not saved us to possess a partial religion. No! God has saved us to be free children of God. He has saved us to be slaves. Yes! But to be slaves to righteousness and to God. "You have been set free from sin and have become slaves to righteousness" (v. 28 NIV).

Bob Dylan used to sing the song "You Gonna Have To Serve Somebody." In his nasal twang he would spout, "It might be the devil, it might be the Lord. But you gonna have to serve somebody." It is true. The only freedom we have is to select the Lord unto which we give our lives. Do we live our lives subject to the slavery of sin or do we live our lives under the Lordship of Christ?

We have been set free. We have been given complete forgiveness. The slate is wiped clean. We have been given the indwelling Holy Spirit's power to say, "No," to sin's control. We now are free children of God, inheritors of the very life of Christ. What are we going to do with our newly found freedom? Free, for what?

Paul explains! "I put this in human terms because you are weak in your natural selves. Just as you used to offer the parts of your body in slavery to impurity and to ever-increasing wickedness, so now offer them in slavery to righteousness leading to holiness" (v. 19 NIV). "But now that you have been set free from sin and have become slaves to God, the benefit you reap leads to holiness, and the result is eternal life" (v. 22 NIV). I think that Paul is saying

71

that there must be an ethical dimension to our faith. Christ must make some kind of difference in our everyday life. I think that he is saying that since we are "weak in our natural selves," we must be free to discipline and equip ourselves to exercise our freedom only to Christ in a way that "leads to holiness." If he is Lord, I am not. What are the essentials that lead me as I follow the Master?

One essential in our spiritual discipline is Bible study. Good Bible study sets before us all of the Bible, not just the parts we prefer. You may remember that Thomas Jefferson went through his Bible and cut out all the parts he did not like! I think that God wants us to read his word in almost a naive way, as if we had never read it before or we don't know what it says before we read it. We are to sit before God's word as it becomes a mirror that convicts us of any sin and self-centeredness. We look into all of his Word to find God's will for our lives. We do not look into God's Word searching for proof-texts often taken out of context, to prop up our own beliefs, or to sanction what we have already decided to do, then boastfully brag, "God told me to do this!" Sitting before God's Word can bring the power of conviction and guidance. That's why we need the discipline of daily Bible study.

It also is true that the more I learn about God's Word, the more I realize how little I know. I realize I do not have the corner on God or the truth. Disciplined study of God's Word helps to keep suppressed my pride, arrogance, and judgmentalism. I wonder if Big Harold ever said, "I don't know?"

We also need the discipline of prayer. When we listen as well as speak in prayer, God keeps us humble. As one has said, "It is hard to have your nose in the air when you are bowed on your knees." In prayer we are reminded that we have nothing of which we can boast, and the only cure for our condition of sin is his grace. We realize that we cannot live life in our own power and must have his.

Elizabeth O'Connor related the story of two men who rode to work together in a car pool. Each day one would ask the other to let him off at a house of worship on the way home. Finally, the driver asked, "What do you do when you go into that church?" The other responded, "I look at him. He looks at me." In the true discipline of prayer, I see him for what he is. In the true discipline of prayer, I see myself for what I am and somewhat of what I can become."

We not only need the discipline of prayer, we must have the discipline of private and corporate worship. It is in worship that we are reminded of the majesty, the expanse, and the breadth of God. Pushed aside are our petty concepts of a puny God who is narrow and confined to our experiences, whims, and prejudices. We come to worship and are bowled over by a God who is bigger than our minds can conceive. We hear of a God who explodes the universe into being, out of nothing, with the mere sound of his voice! Bam! Nothing is too great for this great God. This is a God of all the peoples of all the earth — not just our people, or the people we like, or the people who like us. This is a God who not only freed the Israelites from Egypt but also the Philistines from Caphtor and the Syrians from Kir (Amos 9:7). He is a God who seeks to love all the peoples of the earth. His reason for selecting me as his child is to love me and send me to show his love to everyone who knows it not. He sends all of us as missionaries to the entire world because his son died for everyone. This is not a puny God.

When we wade through the waters of baptism, we not only acquire a new discipline, we receive a new direction. Our lives are on a different course, headed toward a different goal. That new direction is nothing less than toward the goal of Christ-likeness. Our ambition now is to exemplify the servanthood role of Jesus himself. Harold Warlick, in his book *The Human Condition In Biblical Perspective*, quotes Henry Ward Beecher, "Religion means work; religion means work in a dirty world; religion means peril; blows given, blows taken as well ... The world is to be cleaned by somebody; and you are not a child of God if you are ashamed to scour and scrub."[2] We are again born and baptized for a new discipline and a new direction to be like Jesus and to take on his servant mentality. We are again born and baptized to assume a new destiny. "For the wages of sin is death, but the gift of God is eternal life through Jesus Christ our Lord" (v. 23 NIV).

Michael Hargrove tells the story of a life-changing experience while waiting to pick up a friend in the Portland, Oregon, airport. As he was waiting, he noticed a man coming toward him carrying two light bags. The man stopped to greet his family. The man motioned to his youngest son (maybe six years old) as he laid down his bags. Mike Hargrove said that this man literally took up this six-year-old boy, put him in his arms, squeezed him tightly, and kissed him and told him how much he loved him. He then sat the six year old down and gazed into the eyes of his oldest son (about nine or ten), and while cupping his son's face in his hands said, "I love you very much, Zach, and I've missed you."

While this was happening, a baby girl (about a year old) was squirming excitedly in her mother's arms. She never took her eyes off her father. The father then took her into his arms and said, "Hi, baby girl." He kissed her face all over and held her close to his chest while rocking her from side to side. After a few moments, he handed his daughter to his oldest son and declared, "I've saved the best for last!" Mike Hargrove said that he proceeded to give his wife the longest, most passionate kiss he had ever seen displayed in public, and then he silently mouthed, "I love you so much!" He said that they stared into each other's eyes with big smiles and held hands. They reminded Mike Hargrove of newlyweds.

As Mike Hargrove was watching this wonderful display of unconditional love, he found himself thinking out loud. He was surprised to hear his own voice ask, "Wow! How long have you two been married?" The man said, "Been married twelve years." Mike Hargrove then asked, "How long have you been away?" "Two whole days!" Mike was stunned. He thought by the intensity of the greeting he had been gone for several weeks. Mike Hargrove said almost offhandedly, "I hope my marriage is still that passionate after twelve years!"

Mike said the man stopped smiling, looked him straight in the eye, and said, "Don't hope, friend ... decide." And with that the man smiled again, took Mike Hargrove's hand, and said, "God bless you," and the man and his family walked away. The person for whom Mike had been waiting joined him and said, "What are you looking at?" Mike Hargrove said, "My future!"[3]

Dr. Stephen Brown relates the following story. When Abraham Lincoln went to the slave market once, he was moved with compassion to place a bid on a young black girl. He won the bid and walked away with his "property." There was a sullen, angry expression on the black girl's face, because she felt that here was another white man who had bought her and would abuse her. As they walked away from the slave block, Lincoln told the girl, "You are free."

"What does that mean?" she demanded.

"It means, you are free."

"Does it mean that I can be what I want to be?" she asked.

"Yes," replied Lincoln, "you can be what you want to be."

"Does it mean I can say what I want to say?" she asked, her anger softening.

"Yes," Lincoln answered, "you can say what you want to say."

"Does it mean," she went on, "that I can go where I want to go?"

"Yes, you can go where you want to go."

"Then," said the girl, "I will go with you."

We are free to follow Christ!

---

1. Robert A. Beringer, *Something's Coming ... Something Great* (Lima: CSS Publishing Company, Inc., 1992), p. 68.

2. Harold C. Warlick, Jr., *The Human Condition In Biblical Perspective* (Lima: CSS Publishing Co., Inc., 1998), p. 167.

3. Jack Canfield and Mark Victor Hansen, *A 5th Portion Of Chicken Soup For The Soul* (Deerfield Beach, Florida: Health Communications, Inc., 1998), p. 72.

Too Err Is Human

Craig Christina in his excellent sermon, "Between Two Worlds," reminds us of Robert Lewis Stevenson's tale, *The Strange Case Of Dr. Jekyll And Mr. Hyde*. The good Dr. Jekyll embarks on a journey of split personality and twisted fate when he invents a concoction that transforms him into the villainous Edward Hyde. As Mr. Hyde, he delves into every sort of undignified pleasure and selfish whim. But when the drug wears off, he reappears as the model citizen, Dr. Jekyll.

However, Hyde's fun and games turn to tragedy when he murders another man. As a result, Dr. Jekyll is forced to choose between the two personalities. Preferring the good nature of his normal self, Jekyll swears never again to drink the formula that calls forth Mr. Hyde. But on a clear January morning while sitting on a park bench, the good doctor's intentions go astray, and he uncontrollably reverts to the detestable Mr. Hyde. Despite his desire to remain pure, the depravity within his soul was unleashed, never to be tamed again.[1]

Most Christians are not complete strangers to that kind of struggle. Have you ever felt that war within you? You want to do one thing but yet do not. You desire to be one kind of person but find yourself acting out the role of another. You want to love the Lord with all your heart but yet you stumble into sin. Paul did! In our text he blatantly confesses: "I do not understand myself! What I want to do I do not do, but what I hate I find myself doing ... I know that nothing good lives in me, that is my sinful nature. I have the desire to do good, but I cannot do it. For what I want to do is

77

not the good I want to do; no, the evil I do not want to do — this I keep on doing ... What a wretched man I am!" (Romans 7:15, 18-19, 24a, paraphrase). Ever felt that way? I do not know about you, but I resemble that remark!

I bite my fingernails! I know I should not. Biting your nails makes your hands ugly and even produces ridges in your teeth, to say nothing about shaking hands with a lot of people, even visiting the hospital, and then popping your fingers into your mouth! Yuk! I know I should quit. I have been trying to quit since I was knee high. To quit biting my nails is easy, for I have done it hundreds of times. I should quit for good. I know!

I want to be a better driver. But sometimes I crawl in behind the wheel and become another person. Someone cuts in front of me or gets behind me blowing their horn and it is as if I have swallowed a concoction to become a creature I find hard to recognize. I am not going to tell you how I reacted recently when a truck driver literally screamed at me, "Get out of the way, old man!" I want to be a better driver. I should be. I know.

I know that I should stop procrastinating. If you had called me at 11:30 last evening, you would have found me working on this sermon. I know that the Holy Spirit can work on Monday just as well as on Saturday night. I know that I should study more earlier in the week. I always intend to study earlier, but I keep putting it off. I know I should not procrastinate about quitting procrastination. I know.

Sometimes I do not understand myself, but, at least I am in good company. Paul did not understand himself either.

Not only do I not understand myself, but also I join the many scholars who do not completely understand our text. It is a much discussed and rather disputed passage. Some scholars contend that Paul is describing his struggle with sin before he became a Christian — a struggle that was not continued after his experience with Christ. Is that true? Is it valid to say that after receiving Christ that we can just get better and better and evolve into a perfection void of any kind of struggle with sin? I have seen some who seem to think that they are above sin. But these individuals are sometimes arrogant, filled with pride, and act in a condescending way toward others. They often major on minors and live lives characterized by the petty and insignificant. None of us seem to be immune to this temptation, not even the great ones.

John Bunyan, author of the classic, *Pilgrim's Progress*, also penned his autobiography, *Grace Abounding To The Chief Of Sinners*. As a young man he underwent a moral conversion and gave up three of the worldly pleasures he most enjoyed: oath-swearing, Maypole dancing, and church bell ringing.[2] Wow! What a sacrifice! Is this majoring on minors or on reflection of his time? Either way his "sacrifice" did not produce the satisfaction he desired.

Philip Yancy reports in *What's So Amazing About Grace?* that in the churches where he was reared there was a heavy emphasis upon the length of one's hair or skirt or whether or not women should wear jewelry. Never was heard a word about racism, world hunger, or the plight of the poor and homeless. Is our vision sometimes focused too narrowly upon the petty and insignificant so that we miss the larger issues?

Recall the Old Testament story of Noah and Ham? Noah committed the sin of weakness when he got drunk and lay uncovered in his tent. His son Ham saw his father's nakedness and gossiped about his father's embarrassment. Ham, in his pride, was punished and Noah was not. Is there an indication here that the sin of pride is greater than the sin of weakness? Were not Jesus' most harsh words reserved for the pride-filled religious legalists while he ate gladly with the prostitutes, tax collectors, and sinners?

I do not think Paul is talking about his struggle with sin before his encounter with Christ on the road to Damascus. Granted, Paul's argument in the preceding chapters of Romans has been that we are baptized in Christ and raised to walk in newness of life. We are dead to sin, have a power greater than sin, and can win the victory over sin. However, we should look closely at the tenses of the verbs used in the chapter. In the first part of the chapter (7:1-13), the past tense dominates. In the latter part of the chapter (7:14-24), the present tense is dominant. In our text, the moral struggle is envisioned as a present reality, an ongoing encounter with one's preference and practice. Paul is not only talking about his life before Christ, but also there are real dangers inherent in thinking we eliminate the struggle with sin when we encounter Christ. Pride, pettiness, and provincialism are only the beginning of these perils.

Paul is describing here his ongoing personal and agonizing struggle with sin. Let us not apologize for Paul but take him at his word. I know personally that the demons did not run and hide when I became a Christian. The tempter never said, "Well, we lost him. Leave Gary alone!" If anything, temptation became more intense. Our coming to Christ does not put an end to the dividedness and struggles within ourselves. If anything, it rather exposes the full depth of division. It highlights more clearly the vast expanse between the height of our ambition and the depth of our attainment. We may not fully understand ourselves but the lines are drawn more clearly in the constant war within us.

Some might look at verses 22 and 23 of our text and contend that this internal war should be averted because we know better. "You have accepted Christ and you know the law. You should know better." They are right! We do know better. But the problem is not a lack of knowledge. Say to someone, "You should not take that alcoholic drink. You cannot handle it. Look at what it is doing to your relationships, your job, your liver," and they will respond, as they reach for another drink, "I know. I know!"

Scold another, "You bought another new suit? Don't you realize what this compulsive spending is doing to your budget, your credit?" And they will say, as they peruse the latest sale paper, "I know. I know."

Chide another, "What are you doing with that cigarette? You can't breath now for the pain of emphysema. Don't you know what that is doing to your lungs?" And they return as they pack the tobacco more tightly on their Zippo, "I know. I know!"

We know. The problem is that we do not do what we know to do. The problem is not a lack of knowledge. Most of us already know to do better than we are doing. Then what is the answer? Sink into despair and give up? Some do exactly that.

I had been serving my seminary church just a few short months when he came to our little community to live. He was a twin brother of one of the finest deacons I had. His life had been a tragedy and utter waste. He was very ill and dying. He had been in prison for killing his wife in a crime of passion. His brother asked me to go by and see him. I went by and he was most cordial. He lived in a little room in the back of his brother's house. It was almost like another prison cell. I talked to him and tried to tell him of the love and forgiveness of God. I spoke to him of the mercy and grace sufficient and that God would help him in whatever time he had left. I will never forget what he said. He said, "Preacher, I appreciate your coming by, and I guess the things you are saying are true, but for me, it is too late. I'm glad you stopped by, but for me, it's too late." Two weeks later I conducted his funeral service with little more to say than that he was in the hands of a merciful God.

Some may give up. But Paul certainly had not! Paul's struggle itself was a sure sign that he had not sunk into despair and in many ways was a sign of spiritual health. Paul simply realized that to err is human. It is an integral part of our existence before and after we become a Christian. "For in my inner being I delight in God's law, but I see another law at work in the members of my body, waging war against the law of my mind and making me a prisoner of the law of sin at work within my members" (Romans 7:22-23 NIV). Paul realized that he did not need more knowledge, a superior mind, a disciplined body, a different law, a lack of temptation, or to withdraw from society. Paul realized that what he needed was God! Paul admitted that he could not find victory in this inner turmoil through his own devices or strength. He needed the power of God. Thus, began his confession.

To err is human! To deal with this dilemma we must begin with confession. Years ago, a British daily newspaper offered a prize for the best essay answering the question, "What is wrong with the world?" The winning essay in its entirety was: "Dear Sir: I am!" It was signed by G. K. Chesterton.[3] In the Bible the word "confess" literally means "to say the same." To confess we must say the same about our sin as does God. It means to look at ourselves honestly and blatantly face our sin. It means to say, "I am wrong!" I am the source of the problem, not the church, not the government, not society, not my upbringing, not my environment, not my parents!

Me! I am what is wrong — my choices, my attitude, my thinking, my views! To confess means to face ourselves honestly.

To confess means that we cease comparing ourselves favorably with others. In my junior year in high school I knew in advance that I was going to get a bad grade in physics. I tried to prepare my parents for the predicament. "Ole Pebble is going to fail physics this six weeks." I would laugh half-heartedly. "Believe ole Peb is not going to make it." When the report cards were sent home, I tried to preface my presentation, "Ole Peb did fail physics this six weeks." "What grades did you make?" came my father's reply. "Oh, I got a *D*. Did you know that Pebble failed physics?" I squirmed. My father replied, "Did anyone get an *A*?" We can always find someone with whom we can compare ourselves favorably. The truth is there always will be those who have more and have less, make better grades or worse, and are better looking or worse than we are. But what does that have to do with us, really? I am not responsible for them. I am responsible for me. To confess means that we admit that we alone are responsible.

To confess means that we accept responsibility for our own actions and quit trying to buy off God with our good deeds. "Let me bargain with you, God? If you will only do this, I will go to church every Sunday, read my Bible, and visit the widow down the street." The best attendance our church has enjoyed in the past decade was during the Gulf War. "God, if you will, I will...."

To confess means that we accept responsibility for our own actions and quit blaming others! We often play the psychological game of "If it weren't for you!" If it weren't for you I could have, would have, and so on. She is what is wrong with me! He is what is wrong with me! I sneak cookies and go off my diet because my mother would not let me eat sweets. I don't go to church because my parents took me to church every time the door was open. I am an angry driver because people cut in front of me. I have lung cancer because the tobacco company did not label their cigarettes properly.

Have you heard about the "Twinkie Murderer"? This was a fellow who made an assassination attempt on the life of a famous entertainer. He said that he did so because of the high sugar level in the convenience food — Twinkies — that he was eating at the time.

To confess our sins correctly means that we quit comparing ourselves favorably with others, or quit trying to buy God off, or quit blaming someone or something else, and say the same about our sin as God does. That will happen when and only when we make up our minds to do so.

Do you remember the classic *Peanuts* cartoon in which Lucy is down and out, feeling despondent, in her usual foul mood? "I feel terrible!" she says. Linus says, "Well, if you would only do ..." "I am not going to do that!" she snaps. "If you only would ..." he would respond. "I'm not going to do that either," she retorts. Linus responds with exasperation, "How in the world do you expect to feel better if you don't so something?" She blares, "You don't understand. I don't want to feel better!" Sometimes we would rather wallow in our self-pity. It may be a rut, but at least it is my rut.

Paul realized that there was nothing he could do without God. He knew that the road to God was paved with true confession and genuine repentance. To err is human, but we do have a choice as to which course we will take in dealing with our situation. The best choice is called repentance. To repent means that we stop walking one way, turn 180 degrees, and start walking in the opposite direction. We allow God to change the direction of our walk as we confess, repent, and accept his rule and reign in our lives. Paul's statement in verse 25, "Thanks be to God — through Jesus Christ our Lord!" was Paul's exuberant doxology of praise in recognizing God's gift of acceptance and forgiveness.

John Claypool tells the story of a seeker of religious truth who in his journey traveled to see a holy man. "Tell me, my father," he asked, "do you still wrestle with the Devil?" "Oh, no, my son!" he replied. "I am much too old for that! I now wrestle with God!" "Wrestle with God!" he exclaimed. "How can you ever expect to win wrestling with God?" "Oh, my son. I don't hope to win," he taught. "I hope to lose." In the war within, wouldn't it be wonderful if God could win more in our lives? "If we claim to be without sin, we deceive ourselves and the truth is not in us. If we confess our sins, he is faithful and just and will forgive us our sins and purify us from all unrighteousness" (1 John 1:8-9 NIV).

1. *Preaching*. Volume 11, Number 6, May-June, 1996 (Louisville: Preaching Resources, Inc.), p. 46.

2. *Lectionary Homiletics*, Volume IV, Number 8, July, 1993 (Midlothian, Virginia: Lectionary Homiletics, Inc.), p. 4.

3. *Preaching*, Volume 8, Number 6, May-June, 1993 (Jacksonville: Preaching Resources, Inc.), p. 52.

Proper 10
Pentecost 8
Ordinary Time 15
Romans 8:1-11

Cheating The Reaper

"Therefore, there is *now no* condemnation ..." (v. 1 NIV). No condemnation! No condemnation? Can you think how it would be to live without the fear of condemnation? All too well we know just the opposite! All too well we know the fear of condemnation — the dread that the axe might fall, that the gavel might sound.

I recently heard an interview of Sidney Poitier conducted by Oprah Winfrey. He related to her that his young life was dominated by a sense of condemnation. When he came to New York City in the fifties, he found many doors closed to him and even felt condemned because of the color of his skin. Condemned by the color of one's skin? All too often it has been tragically true!

You may remember the story of Abbie Hoffman. For many years he was on the FBI's Ten Most Wanted List. He became a fugitive from the law. Hoffman was always on the run, looking over his shoulder, fearful that he would be found out or caught, waiting for the axe to fall. Then one day, after all those years, Abbie Hoffman walked into a police station and turned himself over to the authorities. "Why have you done this?" they asked. "I'm just tired," he said. "I am just tired of running and I am tired of feeling guilty."

Can you imagine what it would be like to live your life under the heavy and dark cloud of condemnation? Always looking over the shoulder? Always fearful of being caught? This is a life under condemnation. This is a life waiting for the accusing finger to be pointed, or worse yet, one that sees God as a heavenly bookkeeper and is fearful of when the final accounting will be.

In our text, Paul relates that this dilemma does not have to be. He begins by saying, "Therefore!" Why fore the therefore? What's the therefore there for? The "therefore" in Paul's thought always serves as a bridge over which Paul travels from one thought to another and could be translated "as a result of." In light of his argument in chapters 1 through 7, we "therefore" are freed from condemnation and are set free from the law of sin and death. We are able to cheat the reaper (grim, that is). When we act in faith on the absurd notion that God loves us unconditionally and sincerely seeks to share his very life with us, we are set free from the condemning law of sin and death.

Romans 8 is a celebration! As God's children, freed by the death and resurrection of Jesus, we rejoice in the fact that we no longer live under condemnation but are freed to walk in the Spirit. We are freed to walk under the guidance of our Constant Companion.

Paul states in verse 6, "The mind controlled by the Spirit is life and peace." Our lives are characterized by a peacefulness grounded in the fact that our past sins are forgiven. We no longer wallow in self-pity or the regret of long ago failures. All of the past is forgiven and forgotten by God and is removed from us as far as the east is from the west. It's gone, forever! We are freed from its condemnation and are now freed to allow God's Spirit to give us the peace that only he can give.

Does that mean that we no longer struggle with sin? Of course not! In fact, the entire passage talks of our continual struggle with the relationship of "spirit and flesh." Scholars are divided as to what that actually means. Some feel that Paul is discussing the dual nature that lives within us — flesh and spirit, good and bad, light and darkness.

Billy Graham tells the story of an Eskimo farmer who went to town every Saturday to the dog fights. He always took his two dogs, one white, the other black, and they would fight each other. People would place bets on the two dogs. Sometimes the white dog would win, sometimes the black dog would win, but the farmer always won. "How do you always win?" they asked. "It is really very simple," he replied. "All week long I feed one and starve the other. The one I feed always wins!"[1]

86

I used that story in my daily radio spot called "Gotta Minute?" A young lady called me very irate that I would use a story wherein one had mistreated an animal. I apologized that I had offended her and then asked where she attended church. She replied that she did not. I tried to reply as tenderly as possible that she might be doing to herself spiritually that which she so abhorred in the farmer.

Perhaps Paul is talking about the two sides of our nature that constantly are at war with each other. We cultivate and nourish one side to the neglect of the other, and there is no surprise as to which side is victorious. Or, possibly Paul is talking about something that is much larger in scope. Maybe the apostle is talking about two completely different directions of life — dual directions — one that leads toward sinfulness and the other that leads toward God. One direction is the road of self-centeredness, of "I want what I want more than I want what God wants!" The other direction is accepting God's leadership and guidance in our everyday life. Perhaps Paul is talking about two different ways of conducting our lives, two paths for living, dual directions of destiny.

We do know that Paul is saying that we have a choice, like the farmer or the young woman responding to the radio spot. We can choose to live with an unknown judgment hanging over our head or with a Constant Companion living in our heart. We can live a life alone fearful of the eventual accounting, reaping what we sow, or we can continue with the internal presence begun while on Earth. We are free to share his very life here and forever because our sins were judged on Calvary's cross.

Paul is saying, "There is therefore no condemnation to them which are in Christ Jesus, who walk not after the flesh, but after the Spirit." Paul adds in verses 10-11: "And if Christ be in you, the body is dead because of sin; but the Spirit is life because of righteousness. But if the Spirit of him that raised up Jesus from the dead dwell in you, he that raised up Christ from the dead shall also quicken your mortal bodies by his Spirit that dwelleth in you" (KJV). Paul says in 2 Corinthians 5:17, "Therefore if any man be in Christ, he is a new creature: old things are passed away; behold, all things are become new" (KJV). We are now free to live as God's new creation. The past is gone and the future looms brightly ahead.

We are to live our lives, reflecting the love, graciousness, forgiveness, and joy that has been given to us.

This new life is one that is lived out in a new community that exists for others. Our new life is nurtured and strengthened in a loving fellowship characterized by concern that translates itself in caring deeds which were inherent in the very life of Jesus. But, is it sometimes true that the loudest voices we often hear from the Christian community can be a little irritating on the ear or even divisive within the fellowship? Is it true that the outside world is turned off by the contentious attitudes within our ranks, the splitting of denominations, and the squabbles over hymn books and worship styles? I do not know if they are or not! But if so, why? Is it because we don't adhere to the proper creed or theology? Is it because we do not align ourselves with the appropriate political position, whatever that is? Is it because we are not in some ways successful? Some Christians are famous, have glamorous, glitzy churches, and seem to be mightily used of God. But as I look at all this in my very limited vision, there continues to be a question gnawing at my heart. That question is, "Where is the love?" We have adequate buildings, trained clergy, somewhat proper political positions, near to appropriate theology, and some measure of success! But where is the love? Where is the life that reflects the vibrancy and joy of our Lord Jesus Christ? I only may be pointing a finger at my own inadequacy, but still I am urged to ask, "Where is the love and the spirit of Jesus in all of this?"

In his book, *Restoring Your Spiritual Passion*, Gordon MacDonald quotes the wonderful preacher Calvin Miller. Miller writes of an antique wooden dynamite box in his home. The box was made in the nineteenth century and was carefully constructed to withstand shock as its explosive contents were transported from the manufacturer to a place of use. On the lid were large, red and black letters which read, "DANGER DYNAMITE!" "But the last time I saw it," Miller wrote, "it was filled with common paraphernalia that could be found in any workroom."[2] What irony! Fashioned by skilled hands with the finest of materials for such a noble purpose and filled with "common paraphernalia." Created by the loving hands of One who died on the cross to house his marvelous

Good News of grace for the purpose of sharing his love with the entire world and too often filled with the common paraphernalia of littleness, self-centered pettiness, and arrogance that "only we are right" — such sometimes is the fellowship of the church. Very possibly Paul is saying that it is the responsibility of each of us to strive continually to see that our lives, individually and corporately, are governed by the side of our nature that loves and cares for others, reflects the life of Christ, and exists for those not yet of our midst.

Freed from the condemnation of sin, we are not only free to live our lives in a community that exists for others, we are liberated to exercise a certain wisdom that is a by-product of our walk in the Spirit. Paul states, "If the Spirit of him who raised Jesus from the dead is living in you, he who raised Christ from the dead will also give life to your mortal bodies through his Spirit, who lives in you" (v. 11 NIV). Here Paul is speaking about a life that is alive because of righteousness. He speaks of a life that is in right relationship with God. A by-product of such a life lived in obedience to the Spirit is a certain kind of wisdom. This way of wisdom is discernible by those who are sensitive to it and can or cannot be gained through experience or education. It is not a wisdom that we earn or deserve. This kind of wisdom is born of God and is his gift to us as we live in relationship to him and to his community.

Wisdom! My paternal grandfather was a bi-vocational preacher and pastor for over forty years. I stood in the room as my father talked to his father as my grandfather lay on the bed in which he would die two days later. "Papa," my father said. "I am so frustrated. I am trying to get the state highway department to pave the service road in front of my house, but they are just giving me the run-a-round." In a soft but firm voice, my grandpa replied, "Well, son, did it ever occur to you that you might not always get everything you want?" Wisdom! Some people are wise in the Lord. When my back is against the wall, I seek out those who are wise in the Lord to pray for me or to give me counsel.

When I felt that God was calling me into the ministry, I sought counsel from my Uncle Hosea, a pastor for over forty years. "Are you going to continue your education?" he asked. "Yes, sir!" I replied. "I hope to transfer to Samford University in the fall and study religion before entering seminary." "That's good, son," he said. "Go to Samford. It's a good school. I went there. Learn all you can about biology, archeology, and zoology. But more than anything, Gary, learn all you can about kneeology. Learn everything you can about getting down on your knees and hearing God's voice through prayer." Wisdom! With the ability to gain an abundance of information at break-neck speed today, we may be lacking the wisdom to use our knowledge wisely. Wisdom!

There is a tale told of a very wise old woman traveling alone who was joined by another traveler. As they talked around the camp fire, he noticed in her knapsack a very precious stone. He thought to himself that this old woman had no idea what the stone was worth. He decided to trick her out of it. "May I see the stone?" he asked. She nodded. "This is just a stone. Do you mind if I have it?" he asked. "You may," she replied.

He left with the feeling that his future was now secure since he had tricked the old woman. Three days later the old woman was joined by the very same traveler. "I will gladly give back your precious stone, if you will give to me what it was that allowed you to give me the stone in the first place." [3] Wisdom!

Are our lives characterized by a wisdom born of our daily walk and relationship to God? Are we sensitive to the Holy Spirit — our Constant Companion? We listen to and act upon those inner urgings that are of a divine nature. We all get weary of those who profess, "God told me to do this or that," especially when it involves our wallet. But I do believe that God gives to us a wisdom, a guidance or even direction through prayer, his people or his Word. That does not mean that we always are right or never make mistakes.

I remember the account of my wife's Uncle Arthur, who preached well into his eighties and who forgot more Bible than I will ever know. One morning he said to his wife, "Dovie, the Lord has told me to attend the Sardis Revival services this morning." So, they went. After sitting in the empty parking lot for awhile they decided to ask someone why the services had not already begun. "Why, Arthur, the revival isn't until next week," the pastor replied. We have all been there, haven't we? We just knew it was the Lord's will only to find out later it was not. Even the best of us make mistakes as we seek to obey the inner urging. Sometimes we let those mistakes discourage us and even cause us to distrust those inner directives of "the Spirit of God that lives in you" (v. 9). To deny those urgings is an even bigger mistake.

Immediately, we knew we liked each other. I was still wet behind the ears, trying to serve my first church as pastor while a senior at Samford University. He was Methodist, but his wife and three daughters were members of my little church, and he often attended with them, especially on Wednesday night. I was twenty. He was well past retirement age, but there immediately seemed to be a mutual affection. We talked a lot after church. He told me once that he had never made over $1.25 an hour in his life. He had often worked two jobs to rear his daughters and to pay for his wife's three surgeries. He would always flash a big grin as he shook my hand. More than once there would be in his hand a crumpled five-dollar bill. On one particular occasion, that was my gas money to return home.

Everyone in the small community called them Mom and Pop Rollins. So did I. Pop got sick. On Wednesday, before I left for the church which was thirty miles from my home, I called Mom. I told her that I had heard that Pop was sick and that I would try to stop by and see him after church. "Oh, he will love that. You know how much he thinks of you!"

As I left the church that night, I drove past their driveway, thinking about the Greek exam I had the next day and the fifty-mile drive to Samford. I found five different excuses. I did not stop.

The next day when I returned home from school, the telephone was ringing. It was Faye, Pop's daughter. "Gary, we tried to keep Pop from going back to work today but he insisted on going anyway. He fell dead at the gas pump." Harder words have never hit my ears. Sometimes we may err. We may misjudge an inner urging. But I would rather err in doing what I feel I ought to do than not doing what I feel I should do and live a lifetime of regret.

Are we listening to the Holy Spirit? Are we controlled by the Spirit that lives within us?

Alan Paton's short novel, *But The Land Is Beautiful*, written in 1981, tells the story of a white judge in South Africa. The judge was invited by a black pastor to attend a Maundy Thursday service of worship — a foot-washing service followed by communion. At great political risk, the judge accepted the invitation. During the service, the judge was invited to wash the feet of Martha Forturin, the black woman who had reared his children. He accepted. As he bent over and washed her feet, he remembered how she would lovingly wash the feet of his children and then kiss their feet before putting them to bed. Upon his knees, he then kissed the feet of his maid. All who saw were astonished. Some wept.

The press quickly found out what had happened and publicized it widely, and he lost the judgeship that he probably would have gotten otherwise. Later, the pastor called. "Judge Oliver, please let me apologize for ruining your political career." Judge Oliver replied, "Think nothing of it. Being at your Maundy Thursday service was more important than any old chief judgeship."[4] Now, I wonder, "Who told Judge Oliver to say that?"

For my senior year I decided that I wanted to "go out" for the Sardis High School football team. Sardis was a football power, perennial county champions, so good, in fact, that they usually had to play much larger schools because comparable schools were reluctant to schedule them. My father strongly objected to my decision to play football. He had reason. Not only was I small, 140 pounds and without experience, but I also had a health concern which put me at considerable risk. My father even asked the coach not to play me. But I was stubborn. The more my father objected, the more I stubbornly sought to prove him wrong! I would not get hurt. I would show him.

The season started. In the first football game I ever dressed out, I was in the starting line up against the Altoona Choctaws, the defending IA State Champions. Lined up against me was 6-foot 3-inch, 210-pound Bruce McAfee, who 35 years later was named by *The Gadsden Times* as the best offensive end ever to play in Etowah County. I was in way over my head!

But no one tried harder. I would prove my father wrong! By the sixth game I was the leading receiver on the team. Then it happened. At homecoming in the second quarter, in a play where I caught a short pass, both bones were snapped in my left arm. It was over. Gene Holcomb, the head coach, who was told not to play me came on to the field, something he did twice in ten years. As they put my arm into a splint, I began to cry. It was not because of the physical pain.

As I came off the field to be taken to the hospital, I came face to face with my father. I stopped. I froze! I braced myself to hear him say the words, "I told you so!"

HE NEVER DID!

"There is no condemnation...."

---

1. Billy Graham, *The Holy Spirit* (Waco: Word Books, 1978), p. 81.

2. Gordon MacDonald, *Restoring Your Spiritual Passion* (Nashville: Thomas Nelson Publishers, 1986), p. 205.

3. Jack Canfield and Mark Victor Hansen, *A 2nd Helping Of Chicken Soup For The Soul* (Deerfield Beach, Florida: Health Communications, Inc., 1993), p. 30.

4. *Preaching*, Volume IV, November 4, January-February, 1989 (Jacksonville: Preaching Resources, Inc.), p. 21.

All In The Family

How to begin a sermon? It always is a preacher's dilemma as to how to introduce a sermon. I never seem to know. I do know that one has said that an introduction to a sermon should be short and concise and should introduce the main thought that the proclaimer is seeking to present. I also know that it is very much appreciated if the introduction is very close to the conclusion. But, how does one introduce a sermon?

I pondered how to introduce this homily. I thought that one way to begin would be to tell a joke. There is a story about a young boy who was observed by one of his neighbors walking around the block time and time again while carrying a large sack in his hand. The neighbor stopped him and said, "Well, son, I've noticed that you have been walking around the block. What's going on?" The young boy said, "I'm running away from home." "Oh, you are! Well, I guess that sack has your belongings in it?" "Right." "Let me ask you, if you are running away from home, why are you just walking around the block?" The young boy said, "Oh, my mother told me never to cross the street."

If I had begun the sermon that way, I probably would have followed it up by saying that even when there is disgruntlement in the family being a part of the family is still very special. Being a part of the family is something most of us desire. But I decided against using that joke.

Also I could have begun the sermon by telling a story. I have a story. Recently my wife and I were privileged to spend time with our parents. My father pulled out a stack of old papers and with great delight presented to me a check that was written on May 5, 1955. The check was made out to my father, upon which the memo read, "For Father's Day!" It was signed by me and the sum of the check was for one billion dollars. Needless to say, my father never tried to cash that check. He has kept it all of these years. If he had cashed that check and somehow by a miracle gotten the money, the amount still would have been insufficient to repay him for all that he is to me.

If I had started the sermon that way, I probably would have proceeded by posing the question, "How can we ever repay someone for giving us life and nurturing us through the varied circumstances and adjustments that constitutes our rearing?" Impossible! But I decided against using that story.

An additional way of starting a sermon would be to refer to something previously presented in the worship service, such as a hymn, an anthem, a passage of scripture, or the touching testimony of a member of the congregation as he detailed his experience of being adopted by his parents.

"Adoption," verse 23, is such a beautiful word as used by Paul. It is an image that he uses to convey the very wonderful act by which God loves us and accepts us into his family. What a beautiful picture! We are not born into the family of God. We are not a member of the family of God by birth or right or nationality. It is a gift of God's love and grace. We are born in the image of God with the capacity to respond to God's love and his offer of salvation. It is not our inheritance. It is an offer of the gift of God's grace that requires our faith response. The entirety of our lives is a process through which we are adopted into God's family and consummated as we go to be with the Lord or he comes again. Adoption — what a beautiful image of what it means to be loved, chosen, blessed, and accepted by God.

Having been received into his family, we, therefore, have the power to choose life and to walk in the spirit as a child of God. "Because those who are led by the Spirit of God are sons of God. For you did not receive a spirit that makes you a slave again to fear, but you received the Spirit of sonship. And by him we cry, 'Abba, Father'" (vv. 14-15 NIV). Paul states that if we walk in the

Spirit, we are the children of God. To the children of God, he gives the power to put to death the misdeeds of the flesh (v. 13). He gives to us the power to live in daily victory over sin in our lives. He gives us power to exercise and realize what it is to be a chosen and blessed child of God. How are we to do that? I think that there are at least a couple of steps that we might take.

One step we might take in walking as a child of God is to remember constantly to unmask the world around us. The world around us is consistently telling us lies about ourselves. The voices around us can be disturbing, controlling, power hungry, and even destructive as they seek to eat away at our self-identity as a child of God. We are uniquely created, chosen, and blessed of God. We must remind ourselves of that.

The voices of the world around us are not true. They seek to tempt us to engage in comparisons and competitions with others around us. If we do so, we can be led to a false sense of pride or to a paralyzing sense of despair. The truth is that there always will be people who are more attractive and less attractive than we are. Always there will be those who are more powerful and influential than we are and some who are less so. There always will be those who are ahead of us and those who are behind us. We can waste our lives comparing ourselves with others and fail to realize our own individual uniqueness and potential. We can let the world shape us into its own image, or we can let God shape us into the very image of Christ.

Another step we might take as we seek to walk in the Spirit as a child of God is to look for places where the truth is told about us. We need to surround ourselves with people who remind us of who and whose we are. The voices of the world will put us down. Every day they will invite us for a hot, steaming cup of despair. That is why we must take the intentional step to surround ourselves with loved ones and other children of God who remind us of the unique individual we are in God's sight. We can choose the voices to which we listen.

Another step that is available to us along our journey is to celebrate constantly our own chosenness with gratitude. We can thank God without ceasing. We are unique. We were not a twist of fate or a random consequence of an unfinished universe. We are an intentional dream in the mind of God.

One of my twin sons asked years ago, "We were an accident, weren't we?" "I beg your pardon!" I asked. "We were an accident, right? I mean, our older brother was only eighteen months old when we were born. Three kids so close together. We were an accident, right?" I exclaimed, "No! No! No, not at all! We wanted to have our children close together. Your mother and her sister were eighteen months apart. We thought how wonderful it would be to have children eighteen months apart. That's what we planned for and we missed it by one day. Eighteen months and one day! If the doctor had been there on time, we'd have gotten it right on the nose. You cannot plan those kind of things much better than that. You were anything but an accident!"

I hate the term "illegitimacy" with a passion. I recoil in horror every time I hear that detestable word. There are no "illegitimate" children. To pigeonhole or label a child so is a step beyond cruelty. That everything may not have been as it should have been with their parents is no reason to brand a child. There are no illegitimate children in God's eyes. Every child is born in the image of God with a capacity to respond to God, and we hope every child will be given opportunities to be adopted in God's family as his child. Unlike earthly adoption, the choice lies with the child in God's kingdom. God has already done everything he can do to adopt us into his kingdom, and God is waiting for our response. So, we can thank God without ceasing for what he has already done for us. Gratitude becomes the major characteristic of the child of God. As one has said, "God has two places in which to dwell; one is heaven, the other is a grateful heart!"

We, thusly, can enjoy the marvelous benefits of being a child of God because we are secure in the love of the Heavenly Parent. "For you did not receive a spirit that makes you a slave again to fear, but you received the spirit of sonship ..." (v. 15a). Nothing can ever separate us from the love of our Father.

I have often wondered, "How did Jesus do it? How did Jesus work tirelessly? How did Jesus perform miracles? How did Jesus go everywhere doing good in the face of opposition and in the face of doubt from his own family? How did Jesus do it? How did Jesus win the victory in the Garden of Gethsemane? How did Jesus face the cross and all the horrible suffering and shame? How did he do it? He did it because he was secure in the Father's love. He knew that nothing could ever separate him from his Heavenly Father. What God did for Jesus, he'll do for us.

I recently saw an interview with George Foreman, twice crowned Heavyweight Champion of the World. He showed a photograph of himself and another man. He said (pointing to the other man), "That is my biological father. Even after I was Heavyweight Champion of the World I did not know that my father was not my biological father. I found my biological father and he's a nice guy." Then he said, "But Foreman is my father because he loved me."

We are secure in our Heavenly Parent's love and we belong to the heavenly family. "The Spirit himself testifies with our spirit that we are God's children" (v. 16 NIV). Because we are his child, we have direct access to the Father. "By him we cry, 'Abba,' Father" (v. 15b). "Abba" is the Aramaic word for "daddy." "Daddy, give me a nickel." "Daddy, give me a dime." (Or today, "Daddy, give me ten dollars or twenty dollars.") But, God is Daddy, not some far-removed deity: transcendent, removed from us, but Daddy, who is here and walks with us every step of the way. We never have to talk to "Daddy" through a raised newspaper. We never have to talk to "Mommy" while she has one eye on us and one eye on the television screen. No! As a chosen and blessed child of God, you always have direct access to the Heavenly Parent and 100 percent of his or her undivided attention. Isn't that something to celebrate?

More and more I am aware that I was reared in a different time than today. Believe it or not, we seldom locked our doors and I never remember my parents owning an alarm clock. We did not need one. My mother was our alarm clock! Countless times I would stumble in the house at all hours of the night, stick my head into my parents' bedroom, and say, "Mom, wake me at so and so in the morning." Without fail, the warm and clear voice would always respond, "Okay." Dullard me! Embarrassingly, I do not remember the too-advanced age at which I realized that she slept with one eye open and with a listening ear to my car driving up in the driveway. I had her undivided attention even while she was "at rest." That kind of love is certainly worth celebrating and something for which I will ever be grateful.

Paul continues to emphasize that we can celebrate the incredible inheritance we shall receive as a child of God. "Now if we are children, then we are heirs — heirs of God and co-heirs with Christ, if indeed we share in his sufferings in order that we may also share in his glory" (v. 17). Everything Jesus has in heaven today, one day shall be yours. Everything Jesus is today, one day you shall be. You are God's chosen and blessed child — the same as your brother — Jesus, himself.

Bobbie Gee tells the story of Al, a talented and gifted artist. He had two sons. The older son didn't feel well one night because of a minor stomach problem. Thinking it wasn't serious, they put him to bed. During the night the child died from acute appendicitis. It was a horrible tragedy from which the family never recovered. The father's health began to deteriorate mentally and the mother left him with a six-year-old child. Al continued to deteriorate and became an alcoholic.

He lost it all — his home, his reputation, and his job. Years later Al died alone in a San Francisco motel room. Bobbie Gee thought to herself about Al's wasted life, but then she began to think of the younger son, Ernie, who was one of the most caring, loving, and kind persons that she knew.

Bobbie Gee asked Ernie, "I know that your father raised you alone, and his life was full of many heartaches and problems. But tell me, how did you get to be the wonderful person that you are?" He said, "As far back as I can remember and until the day I left home at age eighteen, every night my father came into my bedroom and gave me a kiss and told me, 'Son, I love you.' "[1]

If such love could be communicated from such an imperfect parent, how much more can the love of our Heavenly Parent be communicated to us? If that parent could love that much, how much more does God love you? Absurd, but true! It is all a part of being in the family of God.

1. Jack Caufield and Mark Victor Hansen, *Chicken Soup For The Soul* (Deerfield Beach, Florida: Health Communications, Inc., 1993), p. 117.

Lectionary Preaching After Pentecost

The following index will aid the user of this book in matching the correct Sunday with the appropriate text during Pentecost. All texts in this book are from the series for the Second Reading, Revised Common Lectionary. (Note that the ELCA division of Lutheranism is now following the Revised Common Lectionary.) The Lutheran designations indicate days comparable to Sundays on which Revised Common Lectionary Propers or Ordinary Time designations are used.

(Fixed dates do not pertain to Lutheran Lectionary)

Fixed Date Lectionaries	**Lutheran Lectionary**
Revised Common (including ELCA)	*Lutheran*
and Roman Catholic	
The Day of Pentecost	The Day of Pentecost
The Holy Trinity	The Holy Trinity
May 29-June 4 — Proper 4, Ordinary Time 9	Pentecost 2
June 5-11 — Proper 5, Ordinary Time 10	Pentecost 3
June 12-18 — Proper 6, Ordinary Time 11	Pentecost 4
June 19-25 — Proper 7, Ordinary Time 12	Pentecost 5
June 26-July 2 — Proper 8, Ordinary Time 13	Pentecost 6
July 3-9 — Proper 9, Ordinary Time 14	Pentecost 7
July 10-16 — Proper 10, Ordinary Time 15	Pentecost 8
July 17-23 — Proper 11, Ordinary Time 16	Pentecost 9
July 24-30 — Proper 12, Ordinary Time 17	Pentecost 10
July 31-Aug. 6 — Proper 13, Ordinary Time 18	Pentecost 11
Aug. 7-13 — Proper 14, Ordinary Time 19	Pentecost 12
Aug. 14-20 — Proper 15, Ordinary Time 20	Pentecost 13
Aug. 21-27 — Proper 16, Ordinary Time 21	Pentecost 14
Aug. 28-Sept. 3 — Proper 17, Ordinary Time 22	Pentecost 15
Sept. 4-10 — Proper 18, Ordinary Time 23	Pentecost 16
Sept. 11-17 — Proper 19, Ordinary Time 24	Pentecost 17
Sept. 18-24 — Proper 20, Ordinary Time 25	Pentecost 18

Sept. 25-Oct. 1 — Proper 21, Ordinary Time 26	Pentecost 19
Oct. 2-8 — Proper 22, Ordinary Time 27	Pentecost 20
Oct. 9-15 — Proper 23, Ordinary Time 28	Pentecost 21
Oct. 16-22 — Proper 24, Ordinary Time 29	Pentecost 22
Oct. 23-29 — Proper 25, Ordinary Time 30	Pentecost 23
Oct. 30-Nov. 5 — Proper 26, Ordinary Time 31	Pentecost 24
Nov. 6-12 — Proper 27, Ordinary Time 32	Pentecost 25
Nov. 13-19 — Proper 28, Ordinary Time 33	Pentecost 26
	Pentecost 27
Nov. 20-26 — Christ the King	Christ the King

Reformation Day (or last Sunday in October) is October 31 (Revised Common, Lutheran)

All Saints' Day (or first Sunday in November) is November 1 (Revised Common, Lutheran, Roman Catholic)

Books In This Cycle A Series

GOSPEL SET
It's News To Me! Messages Of Hope For Those Who Haven't Heard
Sermons For Advent/Christmas/Epiphany
Linda Schiphorst McCoy

Tears Of Sadness, Tears Of Gladness
Sermons For Lent/Easter
Albert G. Butzer, III

Pentecost Fire: Preaching Community In Seasons Of Change
Sermons For Sundays After Pentecost (First Third)
Schuyler Rhodes

Questions Of Faith
Sermons For Sundays After Pentecost (Middle Third)
Marilyn Saure Breckenridge

The Home Stretch: Matthew's Vision Of Servanthood In The End-Time
Sermons For Sundays After Pentecost (Last Third)
Mary Sue Dehmlow Dreier

FIRST LESSON SET
Long Time Coming!
Sermons For Advent/Christmas/Epiphany
Stephen M. Crotts

Restoring The Future
Sermons For Lent/Easter
Robert J. Elder

Formed By A Dream
Sermons For Sundays After Pentecost (First Third)
Kristin Borsgard Wee

Living On One Day's Rations
Sermons For Sundays After Pentecost (Middle Third)
Douglas B. Bailey

Let's Get Committed
Sermons For Sundays After Pentecost (Last Third)
Derl G. Keefer

SECOND LESSON SET

Holy E-Mail
Sermons For Advent/Christmas/Epiphany
Dallas A. Brauninger

Access To High Hope
Sermons For Lent/Easter
Harry N. Huxhold

Acting On The Absurd
Sermons For Sundays After Pentecost (First Third)
Gary L. Carver

A Call To Love
Sermons For Sundays After Pentecost (Middle Third)
Tom M. Garrison

Distinctively Different
Sermons For Sundays After Pentecost (Last Third)
Gary L. Carver